The Survivor in Us All

The Survivor in Us All

FOUR YOUNG SISTERS
IN THE HOLOCAUST

Erna F. Rubinstein

Archon Books

First published 1983 in hardcover as an Archon Book,
an imprint of The Shoe String Press, Inc.,
North Haven, Connecticut 06473, as
*The Survivor in Us All: A Memoir of
the Holocaust.*

Reprinted in paperback in 1986, with a new subtitle.

Library of Congress Cataloging-in-Publication Data

Rubinstein, Erna F
 The survivor in us all.
 Originally published in 1983 with subtitle: A memoir of
the Holocaust.
 1. Rubinstein, Erna F. 2. Holocaust, Jewish (1939-
1945)--Personal narratives. 3. Holocaust, Jewish (1939-
1945)--Poland. 4. Jews--Poland--Biography. I. Title.
D810.J4R796 1986   940.53'15'039240438   86-10844
ISBN 0-208-02129-9 (pbk.)

Printed in the United States of America

The author expresses her appreciation to Joyce Dallaportas for her work on the manuscript, and for her encouragement in seeking publication.

1 "The Germans are coming!"
"The Germans are marching into Poland."

On the eve of 1 September, 1939, the news spread like fire through our town. Within an hour everybody was in the streets.

Some people who had a car or a horse and wagon were already loading their precious belongings. Others were desperately looking for some means of transportation, ready to pay any price—anything that would take them away from this border town, because the Germans would come here first.

Children were dressed in their Sunday best, shivering and crying, for they had been taken out of their warm beds into the cold September night.

"Pola, you will catch a cold," Mother scolded. Pola had only her nightgown on and was looking around with her big brown eyes. Anna, small and amazed, was hiding behind her. Mother took the two children inside.

Mania and I remained with Father. Standing on our doorstep, we watched our friends and neighbors leave. I found it hard to believe that only a few hours ago there had been laughter in these streets, that students had been celebrating the last days of their school vacation. Families had been enjoying the comforts of their homes, and children had been safely tucked into their beds. Now, they were leaving, leaving everything and running away.

Our town looked like a circus tent full of frightened animals moving in chaos.

"Father, why are we just standing and watching? Shouldn't we be getting ready to leave? Aren't you afraid?"

"Let's not get hysterical, Ruth," Father answered calmly, but I could see his right eye twitching as it always did when he was upset.

"Why don't you all come in and talk it over?" Mother's voice came from inside. The four of us gathered around the table and talked in whispers, for the little ones were asleep. A moment later Frank, a Polish boy who lived next door, burst into the room, his face pale.

"We are all ready to leave. We managed to load everything into my Fiat. How about you? Aren't you leaving?"

"Frank, don't get so excited, the little ones are sleeping," I said.

"Mr. Bachner," he turned to my father, "don't you know what is happening? Didn't you hear? The Germans might be here at any moment. We are only thirty kilometers from the border. How long do you think it will take them to get here? With all the tanks they have there, they could be marching into town right now."

"You might be right, Frank, but what if they do come? We didn't harm anybody. Why should they want to harm us? Just because we are Jewish?" Mother asked.

"I guess you people don't understand, or maybe you just don't like to leave all that." He pointed toward the dry goods store that was in front of our apartment.

"We are going away," he continued. "We don't care about anything." Frank walked over to Father who was pacing the room, his eye twitching more than ever.

"Mr. Bachner, do forgive me, but you don't know what I have been through tonight. When we heard the news, Father and I went to the town hall. There were hundreds of young men there who wanted to enlist. 'We have no orders; we can do nothing,' the big, fat magistrate shouted."

"Orders, he wants orders, when the Germans are on his neck?"

" 'Give us uniforms, give us guns,' " we pleaded. But nothing would do. No orders. We went home and packed. You can't stay here, please believe me. Even we Poles are running, and there is no telling what they will do to you. You must go."

"Father, maybe Frank is right. Perhaps we should all go away for a while? We can always come back when the fighting is over." I spoke, remembering Hitler's persecution of Jews in Germany, Austria, and Czechoslovakia.

"I can pack in no time. We need take only what is necessary for the trip. We shall close the house and the store until we come back," Mother added.

"All right, then!" Father agreed. "Tonia, give me the

2

money. You get the children's clothes together and put some food into the basket, while I go out to see if I can buy a horse."

"I hope you will find a horse and a wagon. Maybe we shall meet somewhere," Frank said and rushed out of the room.

I followed because I wanted to shake his hand or just say something to him. After all, we had gone to school together all these years and now he was leaving. But I lost sight of him immediately in the swelling crowds. At the end of our block, four streets came together, and this intersection looked like an ocean of people. The moon was full and in its light I could see the Steins, the Ehrlichs, the Koscielnickis, and all the others gathered in family groups and ready to leave.

Father came out of the house. "I hope I can buy a good horse and a wagon," he said. I watched him trying to get through the crowds. How proudly he walked. The family meant everything to Father: his wife, his four daughters, and his son. "There is no one like him," Father would brag. "Imagine, four daughters and then, finally, a son," he would say to his customers in the store.

Mojshele was the youngest in our family. How well I remember when he was born. Every night Mania and I listened for noises in Mother's bedroom. A nurse slept with Mother for the last few nights, but that night it was different. Mania and I prayed hard for we wanted the baby to be a boy. That night we heard Mother moaning and crying, even screaming. The wet nurse would walk around and talk to her. The nurse would deliver the baby. There was only one doctor in town, and he wouldn't bother unless it was a complicated delivery.

Every time Mother screamed, I held Mania's hand tighter.

"O Lord, make it be over," I prayed. I must have fallen asleep after a while, for it was almost dawn when I opened my eyes and heard a cry.

"Mania, Mania." I pulled at my sister, sleeping next to me, "Listen, the baby."

Mania jumped out of bed, but I pulled her back in.

"You can't. Papa will be angry." Just then we heard his familiar steps coming into our room. We pretended to be asleep.

"Mania, Ruth, wake up, you have a brother," he said with great pride in his voice. We jumped out of bed and ran into Mother's bedroom.

3

"Shhhhhh," whispered the nurse. Mother was asleep.

In a small laundry basket rested a tiny, wrinkly faced creature.

"The nurse is going to bathe him. You will see how beautiful he is," Father whispered.

"Here, here is a golden dollar. Each of you will put one into his first bath, for he should live to be happy and healthy and rich," Father explained as he handed one shiny coin to me and one to Mania.

Then as now, Father always wanted the best for his family and so when he saw everybody running away from Zablocie, he, too, went out to try to get some means of transportation which would take us to safety.

Now, as I was standing on the doorstep, I noticed him riding in a wagon and trying to get through to our house. I ran inside to tell everybody that Father had found a horse and wagon.

"Wake up the children, Ruth. I'll pack," Mother said.

I walked into the dark room and listened to the peaceful breathing of Anna and Mojshele. Pola was already awake.

"Pola, get dressed, we have to go away for a while," I whispered.

"Anna, wake up, darling, it is time to wake up. Mojshele, here, look, it's Ruth. Anna is already awake, you see?" I put the lights on. "We shall all get dressed now and go on a trip. But soon we shall come back," I added.

"Why should we go away?" Anna asked, trying to get into her dress.

"I don't want to go away, I want to sleep," Mojshele said, jumping back into bed. I picked up the seven-year-old boy and put him on my lap. Holding his small hands in mine, I explained:

"Mother, Father, Mania, Pola, Anna, and Mojshele are going to Grandmother Bachner for a visit——"

"And you?" he interrupted.

"Of course, I shall go with you. All right? Mojshele will go now?" I helped him to get dressed.

"Are we going by train?" Anna asked.

"No, Father bought a horse with a wagon."

"A horse," Anna screamed. "Yooooo-hooooo."

"Could I sit on the horse?" Mojshele asked.

4

"We shall see about that. Now out with you all."

Pola ran into Mother's room, yelling: "Mother, can I take my books?"

"Yes, take your books."

"Mother, are we taking the sewing machine? I have to finish Anna's dress. I must have the sewing machine," Mania insisted.

"I don't know, you better ask Father. It might be too heavy."

"Mother, I must take all my dolls. I can't leave them at home alone," Anna wailed.

Father's voice came through the door:

"Tonia, children, don't take too much. All we need are some clothes and enough food to cary us a couple of days. We shall lock the house, and I am sure nobody will touch anything."

"Joseph, I cooked fish for Sabbath. Can I take them?" Mother asked.

"How do you expect to carry the fish? Take them to the Freunds, they are staying. Mrs. Freund is an invalid, they can't move her," he replied.

"You know what we could do?" Pola volunteered. "We could leave the fish on the table and put some poison in it. If the Germans come into our house and eat the fish, they will die and that will serve them right."

"Pola, what got into your head? What kind of talk is that?" Mother scolded.

I didn't say anything, but I liked Pola's plan and wished I knew of some poison I could put into the fish. Then another thought crossed my mind. When the Germans come, they will be in a hurry and they will eat the fish quickly, and since a carp has a lot of bones, they will choke on it and die anyway. When no one was watching, I put the fish in the kitchen and covered it so Mother wouldn't find it.

When we were almost ready to leave, Mother suddenly said:

"Joseph, perhaps we should stay after all. Look, the Heinlichs and the Furths are staying. They have been our neighbors all our lives. Can you imagine them hurting us? Do you think the other Germans are different?"

"Oh, Papa, please stay," Mania begged.

We all looked at Father. He shook his head.

"I have to get you children away from here. There will be fighting, but the fighting won't be long, so why sit here and worry? We can go to Krakow, to Grandmother's house, far from the border. Krakow is sure to be safe and well defended. And when it is all over, we will return home safely."

"And live happily ever after," Pola concluded.

"Bravo!" Anna clapped her hands.

"Enough, girls, that is enough. Bring all your things out," Father commanded.

I went back into our room, the room where the four of us had slept together, and then five. It was crowded with beds, but we had been happy. As I looked around, I saw scribblings, or paintings as we called them, all over the walls. Even the doors were covered with paintings. It almost seemed as if that was the reason we had to leave our home—no more room for paintings.

Half-awake, Mojshele was looking helplessly for something to take with him. He soon found his stuffed teddy bear and clutched it under his arm.

I watched Anna picking her dolls from the shelves, hugging them and putting them back. She knew she couldn't take them all but found it hard to part with even one of them. Anna's tenth birthday was coming in October. I wondered if we would all be back home in time to celebrate.

Pola went rushing into her corner of the room. Her thin hands could hardly hold the basket she was carrying, but she filled it full of books. Books and more books. I was sure she'd read them all, but she couldn't bear to leave them behind.

"Where is my *Pan Tadeusz*?" she demanded. "I must have it. Who took it?" Soon she found her favorite book and rushed through the door again.

"Where in the world is Mania?" I asked, walking into Mother's room. She was there, struggling to tie Mother's corset.

"Mother, what do you think you are doing? We are not going to a party!" I exclaimed.

"Maybe you are right," Mother sighed. "I am so used to putting it on when I go out. But how could I sit in the wagon with this corset on? Thanks, Mania, thanks for helping me with it. I shall do without it, fat or not fat. I will take it with me, though, just in case," she said, taking the corset off.

"Mother, you're really not fat." I smiled and kissed her. I took some pillow cases from the chest and handed one to Mania in which to pack her clothes. Father was already piling things up on the wagon.

"Don't take too much, children, that horse won't last. Besides, I want to make room for Mojshele to sleep."

Mother handed him some blankets and a pillow. I followed to the kitchen to get the food. "There is hardly any bread," she lamented. "With what am I going to feed you all?"

"I'll run over to Levy's; give me some money, Mother." I took some change and rushed through the streets into the Levy's bakery. I could smell the fresh bread outside, but there was not a single loaf on the shelves.

"Mr. Levy, we must have bread. What will Mother do? You must find some," I cried.

"Do not cry, my child. Levy will always find a loaf of bread for the Bachners. After all, I have delivered bread to your Mother all my life. You see, I am an old man. My children are all grown and far away. I shall stay here and see what will happen. You children, you must go away. Here, I have two loaves of bread for your Mother. May God bless her. Hide it under your skirts, child, for the others will be angry. We baked all night, used all the flour we had, and sold every single loaf of bread. No, there is no flour left, I can't bake any more."

"You keep the money," he added, when I pushed it into his hand. "Go with God," I heard him say, as I rushed into the street.

Dawn was resting heavily in the air. Thousands of people were buzzing like hives of bees in the streets, preparing for something unexpected.

As I neared the house, I could see my family climbing into the wagon one by one. I handed the bread to Mother. As the horse began to move, I walked alongside the wagon, looking back at the deserted house and the gathering crowds.

2 We reached the bridge. Father had a hard time making the horse move. All around us were people and horses. Occasionally, I could hear the insistent honk of a car, which was trying to pass through the crowds. In the middle of the bridge hung a lamp, its yellow light hardly visible in the crack of dawn. The lamp was moving slightly. The whole bridge was swaying under its heavy load.

Father was struggling with the horse, yelling: "Vio! Vio!"

"Vio, vio," echoed Mojshele. He was covered with a heavy blanket but was still shivering from the cold.

"Hurry up, Papa, get over the bridge quickly," Anna urged.

"The water must be awfully cold. Brrr! I wouldn't want to have a swim now," Pola added.

"Once over the bridge we have nothing to worry about," Father was saying to Mother. "I am sure our soldiers will blow it up to prevent the enemy from going any further."

I looked back at the thousands of people crossing the bridge and at the Sola River beneath it. The waters looked cold and very powerful. On one side of the bridge was a small but wide fall which emptied into a tremendous basin at the other side. The basin spread far and wide and looked like a lake. It would be difficult to cross without the bridge, I thought. At any rate, if the Polish soldiers blew it up, they would delay the Germans and that was all we needed. If only we could get to Grandmother's, then everything would be all right.

"We made it," Mania sighed as the horse stepped down from the bridge and outside of town.

I climbed on the wagon, hugged my little brother, and told him a funny story about a little rabbit who ran away from home. Anna and Mania took turns telling him their funny stories, and Pola, of course, recited her poems:

"Litwo, Ojczyzno moja, Ty jesteś jak zdrowie, ile cię cenić trzeba ten tylko się dowie, kto cię stracił." ("Lithuania, my Fatherland," wrote Mickiewicz, "You are like health. Only the one who lost you, will know how precious you are.")

"Oh, Pola, Pola, do you always have to sound off?" Anna scolded.

"Wait and see. Pretty soon you, too, will recite Mickiewicz, for he was right," Pola insisted.

"Who wants to hear about your Mickiewicz! Ruth, please tell us another funny story," Anna pleaded.

"I'll tell you one," Mania said. When she told the story, we all laughed.

"It's good to laugh, kinderloch," Mother said.

"Who knows if we shall laugh tomorrow?" Pola added.

"Why worry about tomorrow? Look, the sun is rising! It is going to be a beautiful day. We are all together, and we are going on a trip——"

"In the company of thousands of our friends and neighbors," Pola interrupted me.

"Nothing wrong with that. We are going to Grandmother's. I can bet you she will have hot chocolate and maybe even a cake ready for us."

We went on. The sun came out in full glory. In the distance, the edge of our town was still visible. Surrounded by people on horses, on foot, in wagons like ours, on motorcycles and bicycles, we moved slowly forward, passing women with little children in their arms, young people, and old people. All were trying to get away from the German-Polish border, leaving behind home, fortunes built from generation to generation, neighbors, and friends.

"Mother, I want to eat," Mojshele said suddenly.

"I want some of the fresh bread," Anna added.

"Sure, you want to eat all the bread now. What if we have to wander for days?" Pola argued.

"All right, we can all have a piece of bread now. Like Ruth says, why worry about tomorrow," Mother said slicing the bread.

"I want your strawberry jelly, please, Mama," Mojshele pleaded.

"You will have your strawberry jelly. Mama didn't forget to take it."

The fresh-baked bread tasted good. I swallowed fast. People all around were staring at us. A young man was holding onto our wagon, and every time I swallowed a bit, I could see his Adam's apple move.

By noon the sun was warmer. Mojshele was sleeping peacefully on Mother's lap. I jumped off the wagon as a few men joined Father. I wanted to hear their gossip.

"Well, Joseph, I don't know. I can't figure if we are doing the right thing. How long can the kinderloch withstand such a trip?" a short man asked.

"All right, so they will survive the trip and get to Krakow, what then? Do you think the Germans won't come to Krakow? Who will stop them?" another man said.

"You know, Joseph, what we should have done? We should have left our wives with the children at home. Nobody would harm them. At least they could have watched the store. The way I see it, you've worked hard all your life, even Tonia has been helping you. You built a fine dry goods store, you had a future for your children, and now what? If the Germans don't burn it, the Poles will grab it all. There won't be a piece left by tomorrow, if you ask me," the short man lamented.

"Well, come what may," Father offered, "I shall go as far as Krakow. From there I might go back home soon."

The men walked in silence again. By this time, the narrow road was covered completely with people, and every now and then the whole procession would stop, for it was impossible to move on. The going was very slow, and when evening came, we decided to sleep in the woods instead of trying to reach Bochnia by night.

When darkness fell, thousands of people were spread like mushrooms under the trees. The horses were tied to the trees. We took blankets and some bundles off the wagon and rested on them. Mother covered all of us and went to sleep.

After a while, Father whispered to me, "Ruth, why aren't you sleeping?"

"Oh, Papa, so many things have happened. How can I sleep?"

"It's cold. I can't sleep either."

"Papa, look at the moon and the stars. It's so peaceful. Look at the little bird sitting on the branch. He is not afraid. What are we afraid of, Papa? We always played with Carter, Rudy, and Gertrude, and they were Germans. Honestly, I think you old people exaggerate." But Father didn't hear my last words, for he was snoring.

Finally, I said my prayers and went to sleep. When the noise of people moving and horses neighing awakened me, Father was loading the wagon, and the girls were stretching their arms and yawning. Mojshele was still asleep. I wrapped a blanket around him and with Father's help lifted him to the wagon.

Soon we were on the road again, shivering from the cold. The road was very bumpy, and as far as I could see there were just more people. Mojshele sat up crying: "I want to go home; I want to sleep in my bed." Mother cuddled the little one, and he soon stopped crying. He looked around curiously with his black eyes.

"You want to know something?" Pola yelled. "I think Mojshele is the smartest. We should all turn back and go home. Look at all the crazy people running away. The sun is shining, the whole world is quiet, sleeping in peace, and we are running away. Plain crazy!" she shouted.

"Look, Pola, look, an airplane," Mojshele said, pointing to the sky.

We all turned our heads to the west where out of the clear sky a tremendous cloud had appeared. As the planes came nearer, the people began to push their carts in all directions. Some were running into the nearby woods. Mother grabbed Mojshele under her skirt. Father shouted: "Get down to the ground!" I pulled Anna off the wagon and jumped into a ditch. I closed my eyes and pushed Anna's head down.

"Trat-at-at-at-at-ata," was all we could hear for the next few moments. There must have been millions of trat-at-atas. The earth shuddered. Then, it was quiet. A terrible dead silence. I helped Anna to get up and stood watching the planes disappear. In the road, I saw our horse standing motionless. As I came nearer, I saw the wagon overturned and Mother pinned under it with Mojshele. I tried to help her out. Just then Father and Mania approached from the woods.

"Where is Pola?" Father shouted.

I jumped over the wagon and crawled between people to look for Pola. Father helped Mother and Mojshele from beneath the wagon, and some men managed to fix it. The short man, a friend of Father's, was helping his wife to get their children back on the wagon.

11

"They are not supposed to shoot at civilians," he said to me.

A woman with a dead baby in her arms screamed: "They shot my baby, my little baby!" She was crying, gasping, walking in circles.

"This is what we get for running away from home!" someone shouted.

"I am going back. I would rather die at home than here."

"And without the Holy Sacrament, yet," another added mournfully.

Terribly frightened, I stumbled over horses and people—some of whom were dead, some wounded, and some inarticulate and completely disoriented after the macabre encounter. Suddenly, I froze at the sight of a young girl lying face down.

"Pola!" I shouted excitedly, but she didn't move. I touched her—it wasn't my sister Pola. I helped her to her feet.

"I want my mother, I want my mother," she begged hysterically. Her father was bent over the mother, who was saying her last words. She had not escaped the bullets.

There was chaos and misery all around. Pola was nowhere. In bewilderment, familes with their wounded moved their wagons off the road while trying to decide in which direction to proceed. Then, despite the havoc and tension, the dead bodies had to be pulled into the woods for burial.

Desperately anxious by now, dazed and covered with debris, I tried to make my way back to where I had left my family. I tramped through the woods, and every time I saw a young girl's figure, I ran breathlessly toward it, hoping it was Pola. I even ran into a tree. Throbbing pain and darkness obliterated the stark terror around me. Stunned, I lay my head against the tree and began to cry. "Foolishness! What am I wasting my tears for? I have to go on. I have to find Pola."

Searching and seaching, I finally saw her on a tree stump. Sitting motionless, staring blindly ahead, she didn't see me—she didn't notice anybody. She was in shock.

"Father, Father, Pola is here," I shouted, running for him.

Father rushed over and without a word slapped Pola's face, again and again until she looked up and began to cry. Father took her in his arms, and put her on the wagon, where she went on sobbing.

"Don't cry, my child, they are gone, they won't come back," Mother comforted her.

"They thought we were soldiers, didn't they, Papa?" Mojshele insisted. "That is why they went trat-at-at-at, didn't they, Papa?"

"Yes, son, they thought we were soldiers," Father responded. Under his breath, he muttered: "An army of little children."

Father tied the horse to the wagon. One after another we all helped to arrange it as before, and slowly we followed the procession again. Then Mother divided the bread and handed an apple to each of us; for Mojshele she poured some milk out of a jar.

The sun was setting when we reached the town of Bochnia. As I beheld the dear faces of my family, I could see the marks that the first brush with war had left.

3 When we reached the house where a friend of my father's lived, dozens of people were already there. Bochnia was located so that most people trying to get to the east had to pass through the city. In the kitchen, in the hallway, in the bedrooms, people were standing in groups and talking. In one bedroom, six little children were lying on the floor. We put our bundles in one corner and in this manner reserved a sleeping place for ourselves.

In the kitchen, our hostess was serving potato soup out of a large laundry pot, and we joined the others and warmed our stomachs with that hot soup. Our clothes looked shabby and dirty, but Mother decided we could wash in the morning; sleep was more important for us, she thought. While we were all settling down, Father went scouting around. He soon came back with all sorts of news.

"The Germans have broken through on all sides," he announced.

"How far did they get, Father?" I asked.

"Hard to know, but even Krakow is already surrounded on three sides. We can reach it only from one side, and this is from where we are now. They also say that all the young people are going east. Whether they are trying to build an offense, or just hoping to escape the Germans, nobody knows. I think we should start very early for Krakow. Let's go to sleep now," he advised.

As I looked at all the people and the children half-asleep, my eyes wouldn't close. I could see the wounded and the dead. I could still see the woman with the dead baby in her arms and Pola motionless in shock. I could also see the splendor of the planes, the tremendous speed with which they came upon us, and feel how welcome their retreat was when they disappeared. When I watched them coming at first, I thought they were ours, that is, Polish planes, and my world brightened. Surely, I thought, they were coming to tell us to go home, that perhaps the war was over. The war was over, I kept thinking and went to sleep.

"Oh, my aching back," I heard Mother sigh. As I lifted my head and looked around, some men and women were already up, but the children were mostly asleep. Father stood at the window. I walked quietly over to him, careful not to wake my sister Anna, or Mojshele, who was sleeping peacefully next to me. Through the window, we could see the town square. Each Tuesday, the merchants held a market there. They came from all the surrounding villages to trade their farm goods for clothes and hardware. To be sure, today the square looked like the greatest marketplace of all. People from all over Poland had gathered here.

"Father, look, the Kupskis and the Zalmans. They located a wagon too. You see, they caught up with us!" I exclaimed, delighted.

Father patted my shoulder. "Ruth, isn't that Emil? Or am I seeing things? Look, he's right there with that group of youngsters!" I followed Father's finger where he pointed and rushed out of the room, descended the stairs two steps at a time, and ran toward where I thought I had seen Emil, my cousin from Krakow. Surely, from him we could find out how things were in the city and whether it was safe for our family to proceed to Grandmother's.

There was a wagon in front of me and in spite of its owner's protest, I climbed up and shouted with all my might: "Emil! Emil!" It seemed he turned in my direction, but before I leaped off the wagon, he was on his way again.

I lunged through throngs of people and still it was almost impossible for me to get where I wished to go. Masses of people literally pushed me along in the direction they were going, and I was afraid I might lose Emil after all. I crawled under wagons and horses' feet, but the crowd of people who formed a strong wall obstructed any real movement on my part. For an instant, it seemed to be a little quieter, and I took advantage of it. I shouted with all my might: "Emil! Emil!" Pausing just then, he turned abruptly in my direction, and I began to wave my hands frantically. He was now vigorously making his way through towards me, and I did my best to push through to him. Thoroughly exhausted, we reached each other. He seized my hand and pulled as I kept yelling: "Where is your family? Where are you going?"

"I can't hear you," he answered.

"Where is your family?" I persisted as we moved with difficulty out of the teeming marketplace.

"Come, we are all at Levy's. Father saw you from there," I said, pulling him towards the house. Father was waiting for us.

"Uncle Joseph, what are you waiting here for? Why don't you move east?" Emil inquired intently.

"We are going to Krakow. Where are your parents, and where and how are my mother and father?" Father asked.

"They are all right. They decided to stay home, come what may. But you can't go to Krakow now. The Germans have it surrounded; you must try to go to Lwow. Everybody is going to Lwow. That is our only chance. After all, Lwow is too far away for the Germans to reach."

"I know all that, but we shall stop at my parents in Krakow first, and then we shall see."

"Uncle Joseph, you can't go to Krakow! Anyhow, the Judenrat ordered all the young people to leave the city after what the Germans did to the girls in Wasowik," Emil went on.

"What did they do?" questioned Mother,, joining us.

"Aunt Tonia, it was terrible. I am even afraid to repeat what I heard. All the young girls—the Germans ruined them for life, and all the young men were sent to the front, to be killed for sure. That is what they say, but some people say it was even worse than that. They had a real orgy with the young Jews."

"But, in spite of all this, I can't go any place with all these children," Father lamented. By then, Pola, Anna, and Mojshele appeared on the steps.

"Children, let's get our things together; we shall leave for Krakow as soon as the horse is ready," Mother calmly suggested.

"Well, it is your decision. I hope you are right. Anyhow, say hello to my parents. Tell them you saw me. Tell them I shall come back when all of this is over," Emil said, swallowing the hot coffee Mother handed him. One by one we took our bundles and together with Emil, walked to where our wagon was waiting.

"I hope to catch up with the group," Emil said to me.

Mother and Father stood talking with averted gazes. They then motioned for me to join them, and as I approached, Mother asked, "Ruth, would you like to go east with Emil and the other young people?"

I looked at her in surprise. I was speechless.

"Remember, I told you some of the experiences we had when the Cossacks came to invade our territory. Well, I never told you everything, because what I have been through I didn't even want my daughter to know. I hope you will never have to witness, or God forbid, live through such tortures. Please, darling, believe me."

Somewhat puzzled, I listened, but didn't understand a word. Of course, I remembered Mother's stories about the Cossacks attacking the Jews. But what a seventeen-year-old girl like myself had to do with it, I didn't know.

"Ruth," Father insisted, "you should go with Emil. Mother is right. You see, all the young girls and boys are leaving. When this is all over, you can return to Krakow. We shall be waiting there for you."

"She can go with me. We shall join this group that started out from Krakow. They are all my friends. We shall take good care of Ruth, don't worry," Emil promised.

"Can't I go east, too?" Mojshele piped up.

"Mother needs a young man to help her," I said quickly.

"Where is Ruth going? Can't she stay with us?" Anna asked. Once again I looked at Father and Mother, but their faces were stern and unyielding. It was Emil who interrupted the silence with: "Ruth, you had better come with me. I, too, need someone to take care of me."

Father had the wagon ready. As my family slowly began to leave, Emil and I walked with them for a short distance. I held Mojshele in my arms for a moment, and then I kissed Mother, Mania, Pola, and Anna good-bye.

"Hey, Emil, you look after Ruth," Anna shouted.

"Don't run too far, and come back to Grandmother's." Mother pleaded.

"Vio! Vio!" Father called out, and the wagon moved away faster.

Inconsolable, I stood in the midst of the expanding crowd, clinging to Emil's hand and watching my family leave. At best, Krakow was still 40 kilometers away, and I had serious doubts that they would be able to make it, especially since their skeleton-like horse didn't appear as though he could withstand much more strain. As for myself, I wasn't certain how much more I could endure without the comfort and support of my family. Added to this was the fact that in this whole miserable situation, no step was a safe one and no direction was the right one. Enough! With Emil at my side, together we turned towards the east, joining the group of young people from Krakow.

4 We reached the edge of town when, suddenly, Emil pulled me out of line.

"Where are we going?" I asked.

"We must find the railway station. The trains will be much faster. We can't get any place following this procession," Emil observed.

We left the streets of the town and the crowds behind and ran through open fields, only here and there catching a glimpse of a human being.

"Look, Ruth, railway tracks!" Emil called out, but I scarcely heard him or understood why he should be so excited about railway tracks. I sat down on the grass and didn't feel like moving at all. At this, Emil rushed back to me: "Will you come? Don't you see? We'll follow those tracks and soon we'll be at a railroad station. The train will take us to Lwow."

But I was unwilling to get up; I couldn't comprehend why I should be going to Lwow. Whatever it was I was to be spared from by escaping, I still didn't understand why I should be running so much. My head was spinning as we leaped over the boards of the tracks, but soon we began to see trains in the distance. Emil was right, I thought. As we came nearer, we saw carloads of coal, animals, and freight. There was hardly any human sound. Only the cows mooed and the horses neighed as we moved quickly between the trains. Then we noticed that some of the trains had a red cross painted on top.

"Are these the trains that carry the wounded?" I asked a short, fat conductor who suddenly appeared in front of me. He wasn't prepared to answer any questions when Emil asked another one of him:

"Listen, good man, Panie Conduktorze, can we get on one of your trains? We would like to get to Lwow."

"You would like to go to Lwow? Isn't that splendid. Who

wouldn't like to get to Lwow?" the man snapped in a harsh voice. "All these cars are waiting to go there. Can't you see?" They are all at a standstill——"

"But why?" I interrupted.

"The bridge went kaput."

"What bridge? Where?" I asked, looking around, for there was no bridge in sight.

"Listen, you two, I have no time for any nonsense. We are at war, or didn't you know that? About six kilometers ahead there is a bridge. I mean, yesterday the bridge was there. Then the Germans came and bombed it until there was nothing left but a mass of iron. What can I do? I'm only the conductor. I move if the trains move; they stop, I stop. There will be no way to move these trains until the bridge is fixed. You two had better run along. Get lost now!"

I could feel tears pressing against my eyelids, but I bit my quivering lip hard. How could I weep in front of this man or Emil? I had to be strong. Didn't Father say I was a strong girl? My dear, dear father thought I was so grown up at seventeen. Of course, I looked grown up in a group of gymnasium students going to school every day, doing homework, helping Mother at home with her chores, taking care of three sisters and a brother. How different all that was from this madness. Running, running—from whom? For what? To where? I was terribly confused, and now it was dark.

"We'll show him, Ruth," Emil said and took my hand. Together we moved out of sight of the conductor. We managed to crawl under wheels and behind trains until we reached the opposite end of the station. Directly in front of us was a Red Cross car, but we didn't dare approach it since we knew that it was strictly for the wounded. Luckily we saw a train loaded with coal and Emil pulled me towards it. When he found a car that wasn't filled to the top, he began to investigate. He climbed up and extended his arm for me to climb up, too.

There and then I rebelled. He is not going to push me and pull me and tell me what to do. I've had enough of it. I'm not going to climb into any coal car, or sleep on top of dirty coal. To Emil, I said, "Leave me alone! I'm staying right here."

"Are you going crazy or something? We have no choice. This is the first train. I'm sure that conductor only gave us misleading information. The trains have to move, and this one will be one of the first. We can get away much faster this way than on foot. Please, Ruth, have mercy!"

Emil jumped down and helped me to get on his shoulders, then raised me into the coal car. It was so dark I could hardly see the coal, but I could feel its hard, sharp edges under my feet. I must have fallen asleep because after a time, when I opened my eyes, the stars were shining and the sky was clear.

"We shall get out, didn't I tell you? We'll make it!" Emil exclaimed, and it was then that I realized we were moving. The engine was huffing and puffing and the wheels were rolling. I looked at the stars in the sky, and the rolling wheels reminded me of another journey a long time ago. My first trip on a train. It was summer, and I was going to spend it with my grandmother.

Grandmother Wulkan lived on a farm. As far as the eye could take in, the fields belonged to my grandfather. Surrounding the fields was the immense range of the Carpathian mountains. Mount Romanka was practically in the backyard, then Pilsko, and the highest mountain in this chain was the Babia Gora.

I recalled the first time Emil came to spend the summer with my grandmother; I was nine and he was ten. His handsome features attracted my attention, and I thought that he was truly the most beautiful boy I had ever seen. He had beaming blue eyes and a bushy head of hair. He lived in a big city.

Early one morning when everyone was out doing chores on the farm, I asked Emil to come with me into the hills. We were halfway to the top of the mountain when the sun came out.

"Did you ever see anything as beautiful as the sun over the mountain, in your big city?" I boasted, trying in the meantime to catch my breath.

"We have buildings as high as this mountain," he said, sitting on the grass next to me.

How well I remembered the caress of the warm sun, the soft downy grass. How different it was from this cold night and the sharp-edged coal under my back.

"Emil," I murmured, "do you remember the little flowers we picked in the mountains at Grandmother Wulkan's? Do you remember? They were called edelweiss. I think I gave you some to put in your book. They live forever. They never die. Do you think we could live forever? Or maybe not forever but just a little while longer? Emil?" But he didn't answer; he was asleep. Soon, I fell asleep, too.

A sudden jerk of the train awakened me. The sun breaking through a heavy fog gave promise of a clear September day.

"Brr, cold." Emil shivered, as he opened his eyes.

"Where are we?" I asked.

"I see more trains ahead, but that's about all. We must have covered some distance last night. Let's go." Emil jumped from the car and helped me off, our bodies and our clothes silver gray from the coal dust.

Through the fog we could see endless lines of trains. After crossing many tracks and trains at what looked like another railway station, we came to a group of people standing in front of a Red Cross car.

"Where are you two going?" a man asked gruffly.

"We want to go to Lwow," Emil replied.

"Do you have any news of the Germans?" I asked.

"See for yourself," another man said, pointing ahead.

"There was a strong bridge over there. Look now!"

The fog had lifted enough so that we could see a mass of tangled train cars, overturned, in suspension, forming a tremendous arabesque of lines and shapes.

"The Germans are all over. There is no place to run," the short man volunteered.

A Red Cross nurse came by. "You people better get into the trains and rest. The Germans may come to greet us again, and when they do, everyone has to leave the trains and hide in the woods. There is no way of knowing what they might do. They bombed the bridge, but for all we know, they might come after the trains today," she warned.

We followed the group, amazed that they occupied the Red Cross cars. A middle-aged woman volunteered to take us into her car. When we had huddled together in a corner of the car, she explained:

"We organized evacuation trains in Warsaw. We took our children and whatever we could carry. Our men went into the army. How come you didn't, young man?"

"There was hardly enough time to mobilize," Emil answered.

"Well, so far you are safe here. We painted the Red Cross on top of our train. That is why they didn't bomb us when they came. You saw what a job they did of the bridge, didn't you? The trains can't move any place now. Who knows how long we will have to stay here? There are a few trains with wounded ahead of us, and the Red Cross has been serving food to us, but who knows how long that will last?" she concluded.

Sunshine came through the open door of our car. I saw some young and some old people sitting close to each other and waiting. A little boy next to Emil looked up at him, a little boy just like my brother Mojshele. I wondered what Mojshele was doing now, and I wished I could be with my family at Grandmother Bachner's.

There was an awful silence in the air. Nothing moved. Even the infants were quiet in their mothers' arms. Suddenly, a tremendous roar cut through the skies. A Red Cross nurse appeared at the door of the car and shouted, "Out! Everybody out! Hide in the woods!"

A flood of people vacated the trains and fled, veering this way and that, into the woods. Emil pulled me hard, for I stood there staring at the clear skies as they became darker and darker. An enormous number of planes appeared on the horizon. They flew low overhead and opened fire. Thousands of merciless bullets fell indifferently on helpless victims. We were nowhere near the woods when the planes disappeared as dramatically as they had come. People slowly returned to the train, trembling and confused.

"This is outrageous, impossible! They can't shoot at our trains. We have the Red Cross painted on top," the woman next to me shouted. Emil and I settled in our corner, but before we could speak, we heard the sound of gunfire.

"Emil, let's go, quickly." I took his hand, and we rushed into the woods. I lay down under a tree and closed my eyes, rigid with terror. The Germans had plenty of ammunition, I realized, and they wouldn't spare their bullets. Next time, they might even shoot into the woods.

When the familiar "trat-at-at-ata" sounded, I pretended not to hear. I put my fingers in my ears and imagined I was playing with my sisters. I was "it" and wasn't supposed to hear what they were saying. But soon the game was over because the firing stopped. As we walked towards the trains, we stumbled over many wounded and dead. The Red Cross nurses were working desperately, trying to remove them. Many people remained in the woods.

"Ruth, I think we should get on the train. We are still safer there," Emil said. So again we settled in the boxcar, shuddering from terror at what we had just witnessed.

"Do you think they will come again?" I asked.

"I hope not," Emil answered. Yet, no sooner had he finished speaking, when the noise of gunfire was heard again. This time the Germans fired on the woods. In every direction people were running confused and getting hit.

"Emil, why don't we just stay inside the car? There is no use running. I can't stand it any more. The woods are full of dead bodies. At least, here we are covered. Have a drink of water, Emil," I implored, for his face was pale. Very soon, however, the familiar sound reached our ears again. I jumped, but Emil forced me down to the floor, pressed close to me, and squeezed my hand.

"Pray, Ruth," he said.

"Lord of the Universe," I began but couldn't go on because bullets were piercing our car. The woman next to me screamed and fell back. Thinking she had fainted, I opened my bottle of water and spilled some on her face. Her eyes opened. She shouted at me for spilling water over her new velvet dress. I looked at Emil, amazed, then closely at the green velvet and saw that it was not only splashed with water but with blood. When I looked at the woman's face again, I knew she was dead.

"Ruth," Emil murmured. In his arms he held the young child who looked like my brother, Mojshele. He, too, was dead. I began at once to sob violently.

"I want to get out. I want to go away from here," I screamed and pleaded.

"It's quiet now. Listen, they went away." Emil picked up my bundle of clothes and the bottle with what little water was left in it. He firmly grasped my hand once more and together we jumped off the train. Breathlessly, we rushed across the rail tracks, over people's bodies, trying not to look back.

"Help, young man, help," a Red Cross nurse called to Emil. As he helped her to lift the stretcher, I picked up the dangling arm and wanted to put it on the woman's chest. Her hand felt cold and weightless.

"She . . . she is dead," I mumbled. The nurse looked at the young woman and then in the direction of the woods where dead bodies were already piled in large mounds.

"This is a civilian massacre like the world has never seen before," the nurse said. "Even though we have a Red Cross painted on top of each car, it doesn't stop them! Do you think they care?" she went on. "They kill the wounded, the sick, the young, and the old. Civilians, mind you! If you people want to live, go on! Run! They will come back. I know they will. As long as there is one human being breathing, they will come back." I looked at her and at the endless number of wounded and killed. I knew she was right. "You can't help them," she added. "Help yourself. Go!"

We nodded our heads, and together ran towards the bridge. How right the conductor was! The Germans had done a good job of bombing it. Forgetting the destruction and its implication for us, I stood there transfixed, admiring the lines and shapes of the twist of wreckage under it all, while the Dunajec River drifted tranquilly as if nothing had happened.

In the midst of the entangled metal, several people were trying to get over to the other side. Despite the grimness of our situation, they looked to me like acrobats in a circus.

"Do you think you can make it?" Emil asked me. "Come on, Ruth." Unmindful of the danger, he jumped from one demolished rail to another, encouraging me to follow. For a moment we stopped because a woman was walking slowly in front of us on a suspended line holding a baby in one arm and with the other trying to hold onto the smashed steel hanging in the air. Unexpectedly, the mass of iron shook and the woman lost her balance. I stopped breathing. The baby slipped from her grasp and fell into the deep waters of the Dunajec.

"My baby!" The mother's shriek pierced the air. In an instant, Emil dived into the river. He landed far away from the bridge, then swam back to where the baby was floating. He lifted the little one out of the tangled mass of iron. The young mother crossed the bridge rapidly to claim her infant, leaped to the ground on the other side of the river and waited tensely. Within moments, Emil approached her with the wailing baby in his arms.

"She was lucky, it was a miracle. The baby fell in through the wreckage without hitting the iron," Emil said to me as I drew near. He handed the baby to its mother, who was absolutely speechless. He didn't wait for her to thank him but pulled my hand and motioned me to follow. His clothes were wet through, and I could see him shiver from the cold. I took out a blanket from my bundle and wrapped it around him. Having the river behind us, we ran towards where we saw a dim light in the distance.

A silvery September twilight had enveloped our exhausted bodies when at last we came to a farm and asked the woman who lived there for shelter. She showed us into the barn where several people were already asleep.

5 In the morning, the air was crisp, and the sky was a fresh, fine blue.

"Won't you come in for a glass of milk?" the woman beckoned as we passed by the farmhouse.

The kitchen smelled of fresh wood burning in the stove; the kitchen floor was made of cement. At a long table several people were seated, and her little children, who had crawled out of their beds to see the strangers, were playing near the stove, holding onto their mother's skirt. The iron stove gave barely enough heat to warm the bedroom and the kitchen. Soon, a farmer walked in with an armful of logs which he put into the stove. The wood caught fire immediatley, and hot, red flames brightened the kitchen and made the faces of the children shine.

"Have some hot milk with your oatmeal," the farmer offered, passing the pitcher around. "Where are you townfolk going? Day and night we see people running; women, children, young ones. What is all this? It frightens a man. I have a family, too; a wife and five little sons. Should I be fleeing, too? Is everybody to leave home?"

"Stop that foolish talk, Victor. I am not moving an inch. What! With all the little ones? And who do you think will take care of the animals? Get going, man. The milk truck will be here soon. You'd better have the milk ready. The children need milk, even if the war is on. Like I said, we're staying put!" The farmer's wife argued and at the same time dished out the oatmeal for the children. We warmed our hands at the stove and thanked the woman for breakfast.

This was the time of the year when one season ended and another one began, when the trees changed from green to yellow and red. For a moment we felt young and carefree, even joyous.

"First one down the hill is the winner," Emil shouted and began tumbling down a steep hill. I followed. I lifted my arms

27

and leaned back against the wind; my skirt flared and my hair blew wildly. I felt young and free, drinking the air as I longed to drink life. The war must be over if I can feel like this, I thought. Suddenly, my heart tightened. I was at the bottom of the hill and standing right in front of me was a huge man in an army uniform, his eyes as blue as the sky above.

Emil rushed towards me, and as we looked around, all we could see were soldiers, cars, tanks, and more soldiers. They were stationed in the woods, masked with tree branches, their uniforms and helmets the color of grass. I pressed close to Emil, afraid to move.

"Can we join the army?" Emil began. "I've wanted to join ever since it all started, but it seems to me they don't need any more men. The army must be strong."

"Yes, we are strong," the officer answered. "But who are you, and where are you going? You think you can outrun the Germans?" he asked, walking away from his unit. "They have been on our heels ever since the war began. We have not been able to stop them, only delay them. They will soon be here and then what?" He looked at us. "Well, let's forget about the war for a while. It's almost noon and you two look hungry. We shall have something to eat." He walked over to his truck and together with his orderly brought some cans of food, kielbasa, and a bottle of vodka. We spread it all on the grass, and he handed the bottle of vodka to Emil. He took a sip, then passed it to me. I refused, and the officer, whose name was Stanley, finished the bottle of vodka with a few swallows.

"What could we have done?" he continued, speaking and eating. "Our horses against their tanks. Whole divisions of Germans breaking through with heavy guns, moving at forty kilometers an hour. Their fighter planes and bombers roaring overhead, attacking, spreading terror and flames. You must have seen it yourself." As we nodded, he went on: "They had as monstrous an army as the earth has ever seen. Within forty-eight hours, the Polish air force was destroyed, most of the planes blown up before they could even take off."

"What happened to the Polish heads of government?" Emil asked.

"They escaped to Rumania. That is where we are supposed to go, too. Those are our orders. We shall build another offense there."

"You mean not on Polish soil? Are you trying to say that all of Poland will surrender?"

"That can't be true," I said. "You mean the Polish army won't stop the Germans?"

"Unfortunately, that is true. We are finished," he said with his head down. Emil asked: "Krakow? Do you know anything about Krakow?"

"Krakow fell into German hands two days ago."

"Oh, God." Tears rolled down my cheeks and a picture of my family was before my eyes. I could clearly see my dear mother fussing in the kitchen and Grandmother preparing a meal for the family. Mama's cheeks were stained with tears, for Ruth her oldest daughter wasn't there to share the meal. Grandfather, sitting at the head of the table, was offering a prayer for the family to be together again. I could see Father was worried where the next meal would come from. My sister Mania, the chubby little thing with a funny, short hair cut, couldn't wait to leave the table and get to her sewing. She didn't really like to sew over old dresses, but Grandmother had given her some old-fashioned long ones from which she could make lots of clothes for the other children. Pola was probably still reciting her poems and reading books late into the night. Anna—how she must have been affected by this upheaval. She was at that age when a little girl grows into a young woman. I remembered how we'd had to put a stick inside her dress to make her sit straight. I could see her now, looking around with her big, black eyes, seeing and knowing everything. And last, I saw Mojshele, whom I missed terribly; the little mischief-maker with his dark and shiny eyes seemed to be everywhere. He filled every place in the house with laughter and our hearts with warmth. I was hoping the flicker in his eyes wouldn't disappear and that Mother would have plenty of milk and food for him. All during my flight, to these scenes my memory returned. Automatically, I reached for the food in front of me and swallowed it, still thinking about my dear ones.

After we finished eating, Stanley suggested that we rest all afternoon in the woods, and then proceed east at night, as the German planes had been coming more and more during the day, killing anybody they spotted on the roads. He said we could ride in his truck, which of course would make up for the time lost.

Emil and I agreed and stretched in the warm sun with the whole Polish army nearby. When evening came, we climbed into the truck and moved slowly ahead of the convoy towards Przemysl, which was the next big town on our way to Lwow.

Despite the rumbling I managed somehow to fall asleep. When I opened my eyes, it was daylight. The division was again ordered to get off the road and make camp in the woods. Emil and I decided to move on to Przemysl.

We traveled fast, refreshed after the food and a good night's sleep. Around noon, more and more people appeared on the roads, and the city of Przemysl already appeared on the horizon. Two youths walking alongside us started a conversation: "You two, you're Jewish, aren't you?" one asked.

"Yes, we are, but——" Emil answered.

"Then you'd better move quickly. We left Wieliczka yesterday morning. You wouldn't believe what happened. The Germans gathered all the Jews in town, took them to the square, and finished them. Luckily, Leon was staying at our house outside of town," he nodded to the other boy. "My family got a wagon and left, but Leon and I decided we could go faster on foot. Where are you two from, anyway?" he asked. Emil told our story, and together we pushed our way to Przemysl.

Outside the city all was quiet. Przemysl was enclosed by a brick wall. Hidden within the wall were soldiers with heavy machine guns, masked by tree branches.

In the streets, groups of people with bundles in their arms looked at each other, searching for any information that would help them decide whether to turn back home or to go further east. We walked by, listening eagerly to all the gossip.

Already, a tall, thin man was attempting to group a number of young men together. As we approached, he turned to Emil. "You'd better join us. There is no way of knowing whether the Polish army will be able to defend Przemysl, and if they don't, we don't want to be responsible for any Jewish men when the Germans come here. We've heard what has happened in other cities. I have an order from the jüdishe Gemeinde to take all the young men east."

"How far east can we go?" Emil asked.

"We can always go as far as Lwow."

"And then what?" I asked.

"Let us get to Lwow first," the man snapped.

The two young men who had walked with us joined the group readily. Emil took me aside. "Ruth, look, it is almost nighttime. We'll find shelter and some food, and tomorrow morning we shall decide what to do. Don't worry," he added, for tears were rolling down my cheeks.

When we entered the darkened but warm room of Mrs. Dworski, who had agreed to shelter us for the night, all I wanted to do was go to bed and cry. I missed my parents, my family, my home. Although I shuddered at the thought of what the Germans might do to me, to Emil, what they might have done to my family, I didn't want to run any longer. My numb limbs simply couldn't carry me. All I longed for was to sleep and never to waken again.

Mrs. Dworski, a motherly looking woman, sat me at the table and placed a steaming bowl of soup in front of me. She didn't ask any questions, and after I finished my soup, she directed me to bed. Completely exhausted, I even forgot that Emil was with me.

In the morning Emil woke me. As soon as we had picked up our bundles, Mrs. Dworski gave each of us a bottle of fresh water. But when we were ready to leave, Mrs. Dworski urged me to stay with her. Emil should go with the young men, but I would only be a nuisance to him. How far could a young girl run? she reasoned.

"She can do better than I," Emil answered proudly.

I knew that although my feet were tired, my shoes in shreds, my body cold, and I, myself, terrified of the unknown struggle which lay ahead, I had to go with Emil. He was the only family I had. I had to remain with him and eventually return home with him. If he left me here all alone, I would surely perish.

"God bless you, Mrs. Dworski," I said in farewell and left the house with Emil. The morning was cold and the air brisk. The city was still. No sooner had we reached the gate of the city where the camouflaged soldiers and guns were, when a deafening roar and sudden darkness surrounded the whole area. Looking up, I saw a cloud of planes directly over us. Emil pushed me down to the ground and shielded me with his body.

The familiar sound of the trat-at-at-at-ata made my ears ache, my head throb. I was nearly unconscious and could not move. Convinced I had been hit by one of the bullets, I remained motionless. Around me all was quiet.

"Emil, please, please, go east. Go now, quickly."

Emil touched my chin, alarmed. He kissed my face. "Ruth, Ruth," he begged, trying to rouse me.

I raised my head and lifted my heavy lids. Though I could scarcely move and barely feel, I was alive. Emil helped me to get up, but I could hardly steady myself, my head felt so heavy. I looked around and did not recognize the place.

Instead of the machine gun which had been standing nearby, there was now an incredible cavity in the ground surrounded by a mountain of earth. Strewn on top of it were bodies—bodies of Polish soldiers who had stood there only moments before—torn into a thousand pieces. Leaving this shocking sight behind, we made our way towards the gate, as the images of twisted humanity dissolved through my tears. In a daze, I could only lament: "Oh, God, this can't be true."

Just outside of the gate, propped against the ancient medieval wall, his officer's stripes glistening, was the lieutenant we had met on our way to Przemysl. His blue eyes were wide open. When we came closer, we realized that he, too, was dead. Emil pulled the man's eyelids over his eyes and laid his body on the ground.

I collapsed on the grass, overcome by hopelessness. If the Germans had followed us this far, why not farther? I could not go on. Some of the young men who were traveling with us had been wounded, some killed. The rest were ordered by their anxious leader to move through the gates of the city and proceed east.

"You must go East, Emil. I can't go any further. I feel weary and empty. Mrs. Dworski was right. She is a kind woman. I shall go back to her house, and when I feel better, I shall follow you. We shall meet again. I know it. And together we shall return to Krakow, to our families. But now, you must go. They won't shelter you in Przemysl because all the young men had orders to leave the city. Please, Emil."

"Young man, you'd better hurry. The Germans will be back soon," the leader shouted and signaled Emil to hurry along.

"Are you sure you will be all right? Please wait for me at Mrs. Dworski's. I shall be back soon. This can't go on forever," he said, pointing to the wretched destruction around us.

"I shall wait for you," I assured him with tears in my eyes.

Emil was on his way. Without warning, he turned back. As he took me in his arms and kissed me, I was aware that a part of my life was being torn away from me. My cousin, who as a little boy was a dear companion to me, who had grown up with me, and who in those few days of war, panic, and struggle had come to mean more to me than I was willing to admit, was leaving me now.

Grief-stricken and more forlorn than ever, I watched him depart.

6 The sound of rain awakened me on the following dark September morning in Przemysl.

"Well?" I asked Mrs. Dworski as I ate my breakfast.

"Ten thousand German soldiers are supposed to march into Przemysl this morning, so they say," she stated.

"It has come, then. The Germans in Przemysl. Who would have thought they could sweep over all of Poland in a matter of days?"

We were silent for a moment. I got up and Mrs. Dworski close behind me said, "Here, put this overcoat on. You can't go out like that. You don't want to catch pneumonia. You have enough troubles to take care of."

"I am going to face the Germans," I said, compelled to confront them no matter what.

As I walked the streets, there was an absolute silence in the air, not a sign of life in the city of Przemysl. The houses seemed as empty as the streets, and not even a cat crossed my path. Through the open door of a church, I saw a group of people kneeling in prayer. I went in and knelt also. I repeated the priest's prayer, and then with fervent devotion, I prayed for my family, for Mojshele, and for Emil and his safe return home. The prayer so filled my entire being that nothing but God existed. Imbued, thus, with His omnipotence and His tremendous capacity to direct things, I walked out of the church, completely at peace with myself. Rain poured down as I walked down the steps and into the street facing the city square.

Suddenly, the square was shaken by a tremendous roar of marching feet. "Oh Lord, I know the Germans are human," I prayed.

Through the streets of Przemysl, columns of soldiers marched towards the square. I wanted to run, but couldn't. I was spellbound. I expected giant monsters, but instead I saw men, some young and old, others tall and short, some thin and fat. Men who seemed weary, tired, wet, and hungry. They all marched in step to the sound of the rain. For a moment I felt sorry for them. Above all, I thought of the wives and children they had left behind. Why, they were men like my father, like Emil—human.

I stood there a long time, watching. I felt chills all over my body. I was cold, wet, and despondent. I went back to Mrs. Dworski. When she opened the door for me, I put my arms around her and cried violently.

"Oh, Mrs. Dworski, what kind of nonsense was it to run away from home? Why did we ever leave? How could my father be so wrong? What could these soldiers do to anybody? They would not be cruel deliberately. They were just forced into the army, and they look as human as we do. They even look more worn out than we do. I wish I could have stayed with my family," I added.

That night the sounds of marching feet continued to linger and torment me in my sleep.

The next day Przemysl was bustling again. The army barracks were taken over by the Germans. The schools and other public buildings had to be emptied to house the German army.

When the sun came out, thousands of grumbling civilians appeared out of nowhere. This was the end of the line. Since the Germans had reached Przemysl, there was no use in going any farther east. To add to the confusion, rumors were spreading that the Russians were coming from the east, and they might clash with the Germans outside of Przemysl. All in all, it seemed to be safer to go back west.

All day and night I watched expectantly for Emil. Somewhere among the people who had returned to Przemysl after they had learned it was occupied quietly and without any violence, I hoped that he too would appear. I missed his self-confidence and his reassuring smile, and I definitely didn't want to make the trip back home by myself.

When I finally went into the town hall, I was informed that there was no transportation available; nevertheless, all refugees had to leave the city. Mrs. Dworski and I believed that the Germans were planning to fight the Russians outside of Przemysl and therefore didn't want to have an overcrowded city on their hands.

By the next morning I was ready to go back to Krakow. I parted from Mrs. Dworski with tears of gratitude. With a bundle tucked under my arm, my shoes repaired, and Mrs. Dworski's big raincoat around me, I began my retreat.

7 Tired, shabby looking, resigned, the Polish refugees were returning to what was left of their homes. A couple of days later I was walking slowly through the streets of Ropczyce, halfway between Przemysl and Krakow. On the sidewalks, I noticed small groups of German soldiers. Someone was following me and my heart began to pound. As I turned the corner, a young girl came up to me quickly and whispered: "Come with me, but don't attract their attention," she said, pointing to the group of Germans standing across the street.

"I haven't done anything," I said.

"You are Jewish, aren't you?"

I looked at her, surprised, but when she quickly turned into a side street, I was annoyed and wanted only to go straight out of town and on my way to Krakow. "Listen carefully, whatever your name is. For your own good, you'd better follow me and don't look back," she said in a lowered voice.

The girl was serious, and I decided to follow her. We walked rapidly through the next block, and at the end of the town, she guided me into a small house.

"Kasia, w imie Ojca i Syna—In the name of the Father and the Holy Son, why did you bring her in?" asked her frightened mother, who looked at me and crossed herself.

"Mother, they won't come here again. Don't be afraid," Kasia said. Observing my puzzled look, she explained that the Germans had come at night and had taken all the Jews out of their homes.

"There were some Jews living next door. The Germans ordered all of them out of their beds in their nightgowns. I saw the soldiers seizing them by their necks and shoving them into the synagogue. When I heard all the noise, I followed. I hid in the streets, and when I saw young and old Jews coming from all directions, I ran home. I couldn't sleep, so I went back into the street. It was already morning, and that is when I first saw you."

"How did you know I was Jewish?" I asked.

"We Polacy have known enough Jews to know one when we see one. Besides, your eyes looked so sad. Here, try this," she said, handing me a scarf. "You see, now you look like a shiksa. Isn't that what you Jews call us?"

"Kasia, Kasinka, what shall we do with her? What is your name?"

"My name is Ruth," I answered.

"Well, I guess you will have to stay with us, at least for a while," the mother decided.

That noon we were sitting at the table drinking milk. Suddenly, a terrible shriek rattled the windows—a cry so intense and horrible that we all ran outdoors to see what had happened. Kasia quickly pushed me back into the kitchen. She herself ran into town. I looked through the window and saw flames reaching high above the houses. I watched the fire form strange images; a blurred outline of a human body, the vague shape of a head, a group of naked bodies, rolling at first then merging into a heavy, billowing smoke, spiraling into the sky. Kasia stormed into the house and pushed me away from the window. Her eyes were red, her face strange.

"Kasia, you look like a ghost."

"Mother," she ran into her mother's arms and sobbed uncontrollably. "They . . . they . . . do you know what they did? Oh, Mama, how could they? They burned them all alive. Burned them alive, do you hear me, Mother? Rachel, beautiful Rachelka, who lived upstairs, ran out of the synagogue yelling and screaming to God for help! They machine-gunned her. There she was, dead . . . dead forever. Oh, Mama, what are we going to do?" Kasia went on crying.

That night, I slept in a dark, cold cellar. Kasia hid me, afraid the Germans might return. When the sun came out, Kasia handed me a bushel of wheat so that I could help her seed the fields, and together we jumped on a waiting wagon. The air was clear and fresh. The wind blew my skirt. The sun warmed my face. I threw a handful of seed into the earth and then another and yet another as I followed the horse pulling a plow with a checkerboard of iron teeth. The seed would grow, the wind would caress it, and it would form golden waves of wheat. Kasia instructed me as to which way I should go to Krakow. Leaving Kasia and the fields behind me, and feeling nostalgic for home, I remembered the days when my sisters and I would dive into the shimmering fields of wheat to pick the golden daisies and cornflowers. Pola always had the nicest bouquet for Father.

For days I walked, hour after hour. I slept in barns and ate very little. My feet were sore and my clothes in rags.

Finally, after three months of wandering, I arrived in Krakow, the city where I had spent my carefree youth, the city with its ancient stonework silhouetted in all its medieval splendor against the setting sun. Today Krakow's forms melted with the golden glow of the setting sun, but my thoughts were far removed from its beauty. Concerned as I was with how the Germans were acting, trembling whether or not my family would still be there, I reached the river bank and waited until sundown. Towards evening I made my way through the streets, avoiding German uniforms. At last, I came to Grandmother's house.

"Oh, God, help me to find them all alive." I knocked on the door, my knees shaking. "It's me, Ruth," I whispered. Silence at first. My heartbeat quickened. Mother opened the door. I was in her arms. "Ruth, it is Ruth!" All my sisters and Mojshele screamed and swarmed around me. Nobody asked any questions.

We looked at each other. One by one I counted the dear faces, and Mother then told me that every time someone knocked at the door, she hoped it was me. But today she just knew it was me. Mania, Pola, Anna, and my little Mojshele. Grandmother busied herself in the kitchen, and Grandfather paced the room.

"Didn't your Father come with you?" he asked in a quavering voice.

"Father, with me? What do you mean, Grandfather? Where is Father?" Dead silence. Pola began: "After you left, Father took us to Grandmother's. The next day the Germans were coming into Krakow. All the men, young and old were organized into groups and taken from the city. Father left too, hoping to find you along the way. You mean you didn't meet him any place?"

"Meet Father? Do you know what you are asking, Pola? Millions of People were on the road. How could I find Father?"

"You found Emil. Where is he, come to think of it?" asked Mania.

39

"When we got to Przemysl, all the men were ordered to leave the city, too."

"There are hardly any men in Krakow, except Grandfather," Anna explained.

"I would have left, too, if my feet would carry me, believe me," said Grandfather.

"We must find you some clean clothes." Mother went to find my blouses and skirts. "I think you have grown," she said, as I was getting into the fresh, clean clothes.

8 That cold November day I listened to all the news. The Russians had occupied the eastern part of Poland and the Germans held the west. In Krakow, the Germans had taken over all the large buildings to house the soldiers, and every day more soldiers came into the city. Within an hour's notice, people had to leave their homes and everything in them and move wherever they could. All the Jewish apartments and homes in the better part of the city, and even some of the non-Jewish homes, were confiscated for the Germans.

Everyone who was Jewish had to register at the jüdische Gemeinde (Jewish Community) for work and for food. Pola and Mania belonged to the "broom crusade." Every morning they gathered in front of the jüdische Gemeinde and were sent in groups to clean the streets or the homes of the German officials. I registered at the Jewish Gemeinde, too, and received my ration card without being assigned to any specific work detail.

The following night there was a loud knocking. I awoke and with dread ran to open the door before the others could wake up. Several uniformed figures were standing there pointing guns at me.

"*Was wollen Sie?*" (What do you want?)

"*Du, Komm' gleich mit eine*—Besen!" (You, come right away with a broom.)

I slipped on a coat, took a broom, and hastily followed them. Led into a schoolhouse, I was ordered to wash the floors. The officer in charge explained that at any moment soldiers would be coming in and they would be occupying these quarters. I planned to work vigorously, hoping that the sooner I finished, the sooner I could go home. I wanted to be back before Mother discovered I was gone.

Presently, the soldiers sauntered in, and soon the building was swarming with green uniforms. When several drunken soldiers passed by me and stared, my heart stopped beating. I gripped the broom, but one pulled it away and cast it to the other side of the room. Their officer said: "Try to hurry with your work, and I shall help you to get out of here." I filled the pail with water and with a hand brush began washing the floor quickly.

Even though I was slumped over scrubbing the floor, I could feel the men's piercing glances as they ate and drank. Dreadful images darted through my mind.

At last I finished and tried to edge my way through the crowded schoolhouse without being noticed. Just then, a group of sneering soldiers encircled me and forced me into a small room. About twenty of them, intoxicated with food and war, violently tore off my clothes and began closing in on me. They looked like a hideous herd of ferocious animals. In vain I tried to fight them off. They shoved me back and forth. Finally, one forced me to the floor. Another one nudged him away and reached down for me. One disgusting hand and then another groped at my body. I closed my eyes and gritted my teeth. I knew they would tear me to pieces. If only I could die instantly.

Moments passed before I realized that all the commotion had stopped. Warily, I opened my eyes. When I saw their officer above me, I knew that he had stepped in at just the right time. I sought for what was left of my clothes to cover my exposed body. Badly shaken, I followed the officer through the back door and ran home as he watched until I had disappeared from sight.

"Dear Lord, give me strength and courage," I prayed, wanting to believe it was all a nightmare.

I hardly closed my eyes that night, for the next morning it was my turn to stand in line for bread, and I had to be up early. During the previous week, we had missed our rations twice, although Pola and Mania had stood in line for hours. By the time their turn came, the bakery had run out of bread.

It was still dark and cold when I went to the bakery. A couple of people were already standing at the window. We could smell the bread being baked. Out of the houses, shadowy figures emerged to stand in line, but to me they were the shadows of those beasts who had reached for me the night before. The waiting was long and my feet ached. Startled by the window being raised, I fumbled for my ration card and received my three and a half loaves of bread. So no one could see it, I wrapped it in a dishcloth and dashed home.

From afar I could see the door of our apartment open and as I drew closer I could hear excited voices inside. I rushed in and dropped the bread on the table. The beloved figure of my father stood in front of me. He took me in his arms as tears rolled down my cheeks. Behind him I saw another familiar face. "Emil! Emil!" All the memories of our days spent together mingled in the dear face before me. When he swung me around, I felt for a moment like the young maiden on top of Mount Romanka, near my grandmother's house, playing with my little cousin.

My little brother was sitting on Father's lap, participating in this joyous outburst which our family had not experienced for a long time. Grandmother was already in the kitchen brewing coffee which she had hidden in a bag for just such an occasion.

Questions came from all sides of the room. Pola first: "How far did you go? What did the Germans do when they caught up with you?" Father explained that the Russians had occupied Lwow after they had reached it. Mania interrupted with: "How were the Russians? Did they do anything to the Jews? Is it true that they stole all the Jews' watches and that Russian soldiers wore the nightgowns they stole from Jewish women? Do they drink as much vodka as we've heard people say?" Anna added, "My poor father trying to answer all these questions."

Sitting there in the midst of his family, holding on to Mojshele, my father somehow didn't seem happy. In his eyes was something distant as if during his wanderings towards the east and then on his trip back home, back to Krakow, he, too, had changed—as I had during my flight.

Father explained how he had met Emil in the street by chance, and how after the Russians had sent thousands of Jews deep into Russia, he and Emil had hidden outside of Lwow and decided to return home.

"Why did they send the Jews to Russia, and what for?" Pola wanted to know.

"Well, one day the Russians published a decree which said that if all the Jews who had escaped from the Germans would register, they would be reunited with their families. Unsure of what the Russians would do to them, yet fearful of the German occupation, most refugees registered. They all arrived at a train station and boarded the train only to discover that it was heading not towards the west but east, deep into Siberia and as far north as the North Pole."

Miraculously, Father did not make the train in time, and Emil had never registered. In this manner, they were able to escape the Russians and return home, safe but aged from the hardship of their experiences.

When I went to sleep that night, I knew that deep in his heart Father would retain the memories of those days forever, but perhaps with all our love we should be able to help him to overcome the pain. Similarly, I also wondered how I could ever forget the evil images of the night before which continued to plague my thoughts.

9 A wave of unexpected cold weather descended on us, and there was hardly any coal to keep our stove aflame. Father registered at the Jewish Gemeinde without delay for work and, fortunately, was assigned to a coal commando. This was a group of men who had to supply coal to the homes where the Germans lived. Each day Father hid a piece of coal inside his jacket. He also tied a piece of string around the cuffs of his pants and filled them with coal. The coal dust was difficult to scrub off his legs, but there was warm water on the stove.

We managed through the winter. When spring came, our money was running out, and Father talked about going back to Zablocie. Krakow was overcrowded and there weren't enough rations to go around. A small town would be different, Father hoped. Thus, we began to seek people whose friends had returned to towns near Zablocie and received all sorts of information.

"The Germans have confiscated all the Jewish property."

"We have no home to go back to."

"We wouldn't want to go back anyhow because the Germans are persecuting the Jews." But in what way they wouldn't say.

Grandmother was very much against our going back for fear something would happen to us. Consequently, I think we decided to stay, come what may, because we were all together, and there was a feeling of spring in the air. Father went looking for a job and was successful in obtaining one with a salary in a clothing store. Every night thereafter, he returned home content, always bringing some extra treat for us in his pockets. Farmers came to the store to exchange food for clothing, and many times he managed to get hold of a few eggs, a piece of butter, or even a chicken.

"I have got five children to feed," he would say.

"Not counting us," Grandfather would add, a little hurt that he couldn't help in any way.

Somehow Mother always prepared an enjoyable meal, while Pola insisted on setting the table every night as if it were a holiday. "We have to celebrate every day anew," Anna would sing. Even Mojshele cleaned his plate these days.

On the surface, we all seemed to take things in stride, trying to understand that this was war and believing it couldn't become worse. In fact, we were going to be very good about it because pretty soon it would all be over and we would go back home. Grandfather and Grandmother would have their three rooms to themselves again, and we would grow up and live happily ever after.

Suddenly we found that our situation could become worse. First, Father lost his job; all the businesses that were in Jewish hands were confiscated. Then, new restrictions against the Jews were posted; their movements were confined to certain areas and they were not allowed to leave the city under any circumstances.

By the order of the German Command, all Jews were to wear yellow armbands over their outer garments. Anyone appearing in the street with an armband was immediately seized for work.

Confined to Grandmother's one bedroom apartment, we all sat together wringing our hands and waiting in silence. The air in the room was so depressing that one day I couldn't breathe any more and impulsively ran out into the street. I had just turned the corner when a man in a uniform grabbed my arm.

"You, Jew, where is your armband?"

I looked around in panic. In my hurry I had forgotten to put it on. Frantically, I searched for it, aware of the possibility that I might be imprisoned in one of the jails whose number was growing daily—until I found it in my pocket. The German waited while I put it on.

"You, come to work." He motioned to me and I followed. He led me into an apartment where a basket full of ironing was waiting for me. I was glad it was just ironing I had to do, but despite my relief, drops of perspiration were rolling down my forehead. I had heard rumors that in some places, soldiers raped Jewish girls. In others, they wouldn't touch them even with a gun, for fear of "Judenshande," one of Hitler's decrees not to engage in relationship with Jews.

46

I finished ironing and ran down the street, hoping to get home. I saw a truck loaded with women near my house and wanted to turn the corner, when, again, a soldier grabbed me and ordered me to join the others. I looked around to make sure that nobody from my family was caught and then asked one woman whether she knew where we were going, but she only shrugged her shoulders.

We ended up in an army barracks where we had to clean until late at night. I knew my mother would be greatly upset for fear something had happened to me, and when the truck finally dropped me off near my house, I ran upstairs breathlessly to find the whole family waiting and lamenting for me.

"Where have you been?" Mother asked.

"I was out on a date, Mother. I had a wonderful time. First, we went to Sopelki for dinner, then we went to Jutrzenka to dance. Oh, Mother, it was heavenly." I caught Mania and began to dance, humming a waltz.

"Stop, stop it!" Father ordered. "It isn't my fault there is a war on. I didn't want it and didn't start it, either. Where were you?"

"I had to go out. I cannot stand sitting around waiting any longer. If the war goes on, we must find something to do. Maybe we can organize schools or something. Oh, I don't know what!" I dropped onto the bed with tears of frustration streaming down my cheeks.

"All right, darling, we shall think about it," Father said. "But first, tell us where you spent the day."

I told them all the details. Father was furious again.

"Don't any of you dare to go without an armband. They have sent quite a few people somewhere into Germany for just that. You were lucky."

"Remember to give thanks to the Lord tonight before you go to sleep," Grandfather added.

The next few days we concentrated on working out a plan. We could teach each other from books we found in Grandmother's house. In that way, we would be occupied all day and possibly even be less hungry, for the rations were getting smaller.

Our scheme was just beginning to work when the jüdische Gemeinde announced on 1 October, 1940, that all the Jews would have to move to the ghetto. Father sat in the corner of the room, his head in his hands and his eye twitching more than ever.

"Father, what is a ghetto? What are we going to do there?" Mojshele asked.

"Kinderloch, let me explain something to you. This is war. The Germans hate the Jews."

"But why, Father? Aren't we all made the same?" Pola asked.

"Yes, of course. God has created us equal, but that is a long story and I shall not go into it now. The fact is—and I want you all to be aware of it—there is a great struggle ahead. I imagine that being confined in a ghetto will be the hardest experience we have ever faced. Even now things change from day to day. We do not know what to expect and, therefore, cannot be prepared. I shall do my best to take care of you for as long as I can. But I do know that we might be separated at any time, and I want you to realize it."

I wasn't sure I understood anything or what to anticipate. Too many drastic things were happening too fast. My young world trembled that winter.

10

"Under the order of the German Command, all the Jews now living in and outside the city of Krakow will move into the ghetto of Podgorze by 23 March 1941." The orders came by mail, by word of mouth; public notices were posted all over the city. Father went to the jüdische Gemeinde every day, trying to learn more about the ghetto and the possibility of getting a job.

At home, all we talked about was the ghetto, although no one knew what it was like to live in one. I remembered studying Jewish history at school and reading about the ghettos my ancestors had lived in many centuries ago, but somehow the ghetto I was going to didn't seem to have anything to do with those others.

"I refuse to even think of moving to this ghetto," Grandfather kept saying. "What can they do to me if I don't go? I've lived here all my life. I've worked hard all my life. I don't intend to move now at my age, do you understand, Sarah?" And Grandmother nodded sadly.

"Grandfather, don't you know the tactics of the Germans yet?" Pola asked. "If you don't move, they will move you. I've heard people say that anyone who is found in their quarters after 23 March will be shot. You don't doubt that, do you?"

"But what can people like us do in a ghetto?"

"We can always pray," Grandmother answered. "Don't make us so helpless and old, Leon. You can always find work. Imagine all those people moving in at the same time. They will all want to have their homes painted, and you can do a good job. I am sure Mrs. Rosen will want you to paint her house before she even moves in. I can just hear her saying to her husband: 'Baruch, kochany, can't you see this is awful? Those walls are falling off. I can't hang my Swiss lace on these windows. Have someone paint this room, before I have a nervous breakdown.' Poor Mrs. Rosen. Imagine, she will have to live with all of us in the ghetto!"

"Grandfather, will you paint my room?" came Mojshele's quiet voice. "I want it red, like a locomotive that will take us back home. All right, Grandfather?"

"All right, all right. I will paint all your rooms. As a matter of fact, I will paint the whole ghetto. All right?"

During the next few days, we were all busy packing and pacing the room. Everybody made a bundle for himself. Anna still managed to sneak in a few of her precious dolls. Pola had her worn-out books; Mojshele his locomotive; and Grandfather his prayer book. Father rented a horse with a wagon, and another journey began. It was a short trip, indeed, but what a dramatic change in our lives.

The horse moved slowly since the roads were slippery, and the air was bitter cold. As I looked ahead, I could see the far hills covered with snow. What wonderful memories they held of the Sundays when Father took me and all my sisters skiing.

We were now passing the Vistula River. One could hear only the heavy hooves of horses and the equally heavy breathing of people. Other loaded-down vehicles such as ours were coming from all directions. When we passed the bridge, we could see the gates of the ghetto surrounded by Germans in uniforms. Fear gripped our hearts. The stone wall around the ghetto looked formidable.

"They will get us all inside these gates and then blow the whole place up," Pola said sullenly.

"Let's turn back," Anna urged.

"If we turn back, the Germans will shoot us all. Didn't you hear the orders?" Father answered.

"Together, we shall enter the Gates of Hell," Pola recited.

11 The streets inside the ghetto walls looked the same as other streets in the city, except for the hundreds of tightly packed wagons and the thousands of people who were walking around looking for the rooms assigned to them.

We stopped at the relocation office of the jüdische Gemeinde and received our assignments. After dropping off Grandfather and Grandmother at the room designated for them, we proceeded to our own quarters.

We found the room large and airy. "How fortunate, we have our own kitchen," Mother exclaimed, as we walked in. Pola tried all the doors around the kitchen hoping to find an adjoining bedroom, but all the doors were tightly locked.

"You mean, this is it, Father? Well, at least we have a stove to keep us warm." Pola shrugged and went down to help carry the bundles. Mania and I brought up a mattress, and Mother directed us to place it in a far corner of the kitchen. All the mattresses were placed there on the floor one next to another.

"I sleep with Mama and Papa," Mojshele said, as we were laying the mattress down.

"I have news for you: you will sleep with all of us," Anna said.

"Yes, Mojshele, my son, isn't it wonderful? We shall all sleep together. One big bed, right here along the wall," Mother said, stretching a sheet over the mattresses. Mania and I unpacked the pots and pans and placed them on and around the stove.

Father lit the stove immediately, for the room was cold. Apparently, the people who had lived in this house before had stored enough wood to last for a while. The same stove was to be used for cooking as well as keeping us warm.

Although the wood crackled in the stove and the room grew warmer, I shivered. I wanted to close my eyes and wake up back home in Zablocie where it was always warm and cheerful, where we were happy. Now we lived in a one-room dwelling. Food had become our main concern, and we were learning to live on less and less. The only time I had had thoughts about food at home was to decide what kind of ice cream I would rather have, chocolate or vanilla. Mother used to make it and we all helped to roll the machine for hours. How often we opened it before to scoop out the luscious, sweet liquid before Mother appeared, scolded us, and finished making the ice cream herself. Nowadays, Mother had a hard time getting a few potatoes for our dinner. And all because of the war.

"Wasn't war for soldiers?" I thought. "What kind of a war was this, a war with Jews? Oh no, that couldn't be. One cannot fight a religion. What would be the use? All right, so the Jews of Krakow and the surrounding cities will all die. Does that mean that Judaism in the world will die? Of course not. There are Jews everywhere. There are Jews in Palestine, there are Jews in America, there are Jews in other countries of Europe. Aren't they going to help us? Aren't they going to protest and stop Hitler from fighting us? Of course they are! Only, we have to wait a little longer."

"Mother, why does Hitler want to kill the Jews?"

"Who said Hitler wants to kill the Jews? Nobody has been killed yet!" Mother answered frowning. "Please, put a clean tablecloth on the table, honey, and we shall eat."

Mother boiled a pot of potato soup and when we had gathered to eat, Father prayed: "May the Lord help us to live, to work, to eat, and to survive the war." Mother added quickly: ". . . and not to hate our enemy."

After the first day or two, some men received passes to work in town. Those whose businesses had been completely taken over by the Germans found work in other stores and factories. In the evening, all came back to the ghetto. The jüdische Gemeinde issued coupons to each family which could be exchanged for food. There were several stores throughout the ghetto, and we could get as much food as the coupons allowed. We were fortunate because being a family of seven, we received quite a bit of bread, potatoes, and sugar. In the beginning we even were allowed some flour and once a month one egg per person. Seven eggs would enable us to prepare—or so it seemed to us now—a variety of splendid dishes.

Mojshele was a skinny boy and Mother worried about him. She managed to give him a little extra food. Pola taught him to read and write, and soon he, too, recited *Pan Tadeusz*, loud and clear.

"Pola, please, I beg of you, will you stop? I can't hear it any more. It comes out of my ears and nose. Besides, I would like to read a book. Mother, please tell Pola to stop," Anna would plead. But Pola went on and so did Anna. In some ways, to be sure, life seemed like home, if it hadn't been for the crowded quarters and the difficulty of climbing into one big bed at night.

One day Father left the house in the morning as usual to go to work. A few minutes later he was back. His face was ashen, his eye twitching. "The gates are closed. The ghetto has been closed. We cannot go out any more."

"How are we going to live? You must be mistaken, Father!" Mania exclaimed. Father shook his head.

"Didn't I tell you? They have us all closed in here. They will slaughter us any day," Pola yelled.

"They will starve us to death!" Mania screamed.

"We have managed until now and we shall still manage," Mother said. "The Polish people will bring us food."

"The Polaks! Mother, you make me laugh," Pola cried. "Oh, yes, we saw how they all came out to help when the children were crying in the streets on the way to the ghetto. We were free then. They could have come and at least taken the little children and saved them from this hell. Did you see how willingly they came to our aid? Yes, they were all dying to help, hiding behind their curtains. They didn't want any part of us. You'd better face it, Mother, nobody cares for us, not the Germans, not the Poles, not the whole stupid world put together, not even your Almighty God!"

I didn't know how to calm Pola or what to say to her. Mother put her arms around her, but Pola kept crying hysterically.

12 The first Monday morning in April every able-bodied person in the ghetto had to appear on Limanowska Street. Thousands of men and women were divided into different working groups. Everyone was instructed that the Germans needed uniforms, guns, and other war equipment and that Jews would have to make them. Pola, Mania, Anna, and I managed to stay in one group. Every morning thereafter, under heavy guard, we left the ghetto to work in a tool factory. The foreman at the factory explained how to operate the machinery. "If you want to eat, you must work," was his motto. And so, anxious to earn our meal, we worked intensively, that is, when the guards were watching. The minute they looked away, a worker would move like a turtle. It was funny to watch some machines, at one moment moving fast then suddenly slowly. We all played this game expertly after a little practice.

Meanwhile, Father kept his job in the office of the Jewish Police, and Mother was permitted to stay home and take care of Mojshele.

One month after the gates of the ghetto were closed, our coupons for sugar and eggs were cut off. Our allotment of food became smaller; naturally, the less we had to eat the more we talked about food.

One day at work I suggested that we have a party. Several girls put together what rations we had. Esther had an apple, Sophia had a piece of meat, which her husband Aron had smuggled into the ghetto. Aron was allowed to go out of the ghetto on a special pass, as he owned a leather factory, and so far the German Commissar hadn't found a replacement for him. Pola had a necklace which we quickly decided had to be sacrificed for some flour. We traded the necklace for about a pound of flour to a Polish woman who worked in the office. When the guards went to lunch, we all gathered together and mixed the ingredients. "Ruth, you go and get the frying pan," Mania suggested.

"All right, but what if they catch me?"

"Don't be silly, they've never caught you before," Sophia urged.

The Germans were forever frying eggs, so much so that it seemed they wanted to eat all the eggs we had in Poland. We often wondered whether the chickens in Germany laid any. The guards fried their eggs in a large pan in the office. I took my shoes off and crept into the room. On the shelf was the frying pan and next to it, I noticed two beautiful, white eggs. I didn't hesitate for a moment. The guards were sitting at the table, some of them half asleep. They were a poor sight, those German guards. Old and crippled men, who couldn't be any use at the front any more, so they had been sent to fight the Jews.

Certainly, the idea of escaping crossed my mind many times on the way to and from work, but I couldn't work out a scheme where all four of us could escape. Besides, even if we succeeded, the fear of what they might do to Mojshele or Mother and Father made my whole body shiver. A few people, it is true, had successfully escaped from the ghetto, but their families had been taken into custody, and nobody knew where they were. At any rate, even if I escaped, I wouldn't know where to go. Nobody was eager to hide a Jew.

I glanced at this snoring bunch of old men, trying not to feel sorry for them. When I was safely back in the workshop, I broke two eggs into the batter which Sophia then expertly rolled into a thin dough. After she placed the dough into the frying pan, I sliced the apple and covered it with another layer of dough.

As soon as the smell of the strudel frying on top of an electric iron, spread throughout the factory, the German watch-hounds came sniffing around. On a signal from our end of the hall, the girls at the other end started singing: "Jeszcze Polska nie zginela, póki my żyjemy." (Poland won't die as long as we live.) And then went on: "Jeszcze Polska nie zginela póki strudel w garku, jak się strudel ugotóje, zjemy po kawalku." (Poland won't die as long as the strudel is cooking. When the strudel is ready, we shall all eat a piece.)

The German hounds started to growl and bark. But they couldn't keep us quiet. They knew we were teasing them. As soon as one group stopped singing, the other one began, until the strudel was ready. Before we left for the ghetto that night, we divided the strudel, and its heavenly taste was bliss indeed.

13 One day on the way home to the ghetto, Sophia turned to me: "Ruth, I . . . I would like to tell you something, but it must be a secret, definitely a secret, do you understand?"

"Yes, of course," I assured her. "You should know by now that to tell me something is like throwing it into a deep well. You know you can trust me."

I admit I was frightened, for Sophia looked very small and unhappy. Her eyes now were tinged with tears as her hand clenched mine.

"Sophia, please, it can't be that bad. Tell me. How can I help?"

She burst into tears, wiping them quickly so the guards wouldn't notice. "Oh no, I can't tell you. I can't tell anybody. I just want to die," she wept.

We soon neared her house, and on parting, she looked at me, distressed. The next few days Sophia was absent from work. I was puzzled but was afraid to ask even her other friends what had happened, and I did not have time to stop at her home. On Sunday, I made my way, apprehensively, to see her.

The door was opened by Mark, a schoolmate of Sophia's husband, Aron, who lived with them. Together the young men studied at night, hoping that soon they could return to school and finish engineering. My heart leaped as I scanned the small room. I saw only Aron; Sophia was not there.

"Sophia?" I asked Aron.

"She is all right," he answered, studying me with his big, dark eyes.

"Where is she?" At this, Aron moved aside a heavy drapery that partitioned the room; there I saw Sophia lying in bed.

Aron left us alone. For some reason, I felt like brushing her long braids, wiping her face, taking care of her. She looked pale, almost transparent, and very tiny. She took my hand in hers and began slowly, quietly. "Remember that day when I was going to tell you my secret? You were the only one I really wanted to tell, but I was so scared. You didn't notice anything either? How lucky I was. Ruth, brace yourself, my dear friend. I had a baby four days ago."

"Oh, Sophia, Zosinka, Kochana. How are you feeling? Where is the baby? Where is she, or is it a he?" I kissed Sophia, plumped the pillow under her head, and finally I understood. I understood her uneasiness at the time, her haste always to get home. Yet, I still didn't remember her having a large belly as Mother had had with Mojshele.

"How did you hide carrying a baby from us, from everyone, all this time?"

"It was easy. With the food rations we get, I could never get fat."

"Where is the baby now? Can I see it?" I was dying to hold the little creature in my arms.

"The baby; how I wish I could show you my little Tania. She was so beautiful, Ruth, really, truly, beautiful."

My heart sank. "You mean?"

"No, my dear, she is all right. You know she would have no chance in the ghetto. We had to give her away. When we knew I was pregnant, Aron talked to a Polish woman who worked in his place. She has a grown daughter living in Warsaw. She could say that Tania was her daughter's child and she had to bring her up because her daughter is working. Well, it wasn't easy to convince her; it took all the money we had saved. Finally, she agreed. She will take care of the baby for us until the war is over."

"But, Sophia, my dear, how did you manage to give her the baby with all the guards at the gate these days?"

"It was hard, believe me. I think it was the most trying moment of my life."

"Please don't cry, Sophia," I kissed her tenderly.

"Aron bought off the guards," she began. "He gave each of them a few zlotys so they would let him hand a bag of clothes to this Polish woman who works for him; she, in exchange, would give him a loaf of bread. We waited at the gate, shaking with fear and praying that the woman would come on time, before the guards changed. Aron carried the laundry bag that contained the most precious possession we ever had. As each moment passed, I longed more and more to hold it with him, cuddle it, you understand, but I restrained myself, and only looked at the bag, hoping the baby wouldn't wake up, begin to cry, or worse, suffocate. We had given her a sedative which one of the doctors in the hospital had given to Aron. Imagine, only two days old. My little Tania went to sleep like a lamb. We wrapped her in blankets. I hope she was warm enough. I wanted so much to hold on to her a little longer, and all the while I prayed that Mrs. Wojciechowa would come soon, before I died of fear.

"At last, she arrived; Aron hurried to the gate. He handed her the bag; she handed him a loaf of bread—a simple exchange. A few passersby looked hungrily at the loaf of bread. Ruth, how can I explain? I was standing there paralyzed. At one moment, I was frightened she was going to drop the bag and my Tania would die. In the next moment, I was going to rush to her, grab the bag, and take it home. Then I would take my baby in my arms . . . feed her . . . and love her . . . she is mine, mine! Ruth, our own little baby, mine and Aron's. Our Tania . . . please forgive me," her voice weakly trailed off.

"Sophia, darling, you couldn't do anything else. You know you couldn't keep the baby in this hell. You and Aron both have to go to work. Who would take care of her? Besides, you know the Germans don't want any new babies in the ghetto, although how this will be possible to avoid, I don't know."

"Yes, so I hear. But so far the Germans haven't punished anyone for having babies. After all, we are human. And married people do have babies. No one, not even they, can stop that," Sophia wailed. "Only Aron thought that there is always a first time. You never know what they will come up with next. We just couldn't risk sacrificing our baby. If all goes well, we shall have her back someday."

"I think Aron was right in his decision," I said. After kissing Sophia, I returned home. On the next Monday, Sophia came back to work. Once in a while, she would tell me that Aron had news, that the baby was fine and growing well. Soon, however, all individual passes were cancelled and neither Aron nor anyone else, for that matter, could get out. Thereafter, there was no communication whatsoever about the baby.

14 An intolerably long, cold winter was coming to an end. Soon, we were certain, the light shed by the dim, wintry sun would yield to the freshness of spring. But all of us worried when we saw Father, in particular, becoming more depressed each day. "Kinderloch, one year has passed since we passed through these ghetto walls. The situation, to be truthful, is bleak, very bleak," he would say. At this, Mother would promptly try to cheer him up:

"We are alive, aren't we? We aren't starving, are we? Or perhaps the meals I prepare aren't good enough any more? Don't despair, Joseph, God will watch over us; the war can't last forever."

"The war can't last forever." I echoed Mother's thoughts; yet, the news was vague. Every now and then someone would smuggle in a newspaper, but what good did it do? From the headlines to the bottom of the page, victories by the German troops were described and the Germans hailed. Nobody believed what the paper said; therefore, the people in the ghetto made their own news. When the weather was good and we received our food rations, the Germans were winning the war. On the other hand, if the weather was bad and we were hungry, or the Germans didn't give us our rations, we believed they were losing.

Every day, under guard, we marched to the factory outside the ghetto walls. At six o'clock, when the work was finished, the gates opened to swallow us again. Each and every time I passed through the gate, a stab of pain went through my heart. Would I find my parents and Mojshele at home? Mojshele was our greatest worry right now. He was too young for work, and the Germans expected everybody in the ghetto to work for their supper. My cousin Lily had a small daughter who was seven years old, a little younger than Mojshele. She would drop her off at our house before she went to work, and Bronia would play with Mojshele. In his childish way, he even taught her how to read.

One Sunday morning before dawn, a policeman came to Lily's door. She tried to shush him, for small, golden-haired Bronia was asleep. She was asked to take her child out of bed and follow the policeman to Plac Zgody where several women were already standing with their little ones. Some held their babies in their arms, others let the children hold onto their skirts.

"Why did they select us?" Lily asked her friend.

"What do they want of us?" the other one asked, pointing to several armed guards standing around the square.

Lily looked up at the windows of the houses surrounding the Plac Zgody, but neither outside nor inside the ghetto was there any sign that anyone noticed what was taking place in that early dawn.

"Maybe, they will take us away from this hell and let us go somewhere where our children can have air and enough food to eat," Lily consoled her friend shivering in the wintry air.

Naturally, the children became restless as more and more were herded into the square from all sides of the ghetto.

"I wish you would have let me wear my new dress, Mama," Bronia chirped. "You know, the one Papa brought for me from his store."

"And I wish Papa was here with us; he would know what to do," Lily answered.

"Don't cry, Mama. If we go on a trip, maybe we shall meet Papa."

"Yes, of course, why didn't I think about that," Lily answered aloud. In her mind, however, she was recalling that her husband had been sent away with a transport only a fortnight ago. It might be possible.

A quick, unexpected movement of the guards startled them. Mothers with infants in their arms, babies who were at the age when they had just begun to crawl, and children who were mostly under eight years of age were pressed towards the inner wall of the ghetto. In front of them an impenetrable gray wall of stone—in back of them another insurmountable green wall of armed men.

"Lassen Sie die Kinder stehen!" (Let the children stand by themselves!) the Germans shouted, trying to pull the mothers away.

Lily held her small daughter tightly in her arms. One of the soldiers struggled to take the child away from her and furiously thrust her to ground, pulling the child free with a final wrench. Dashing headlong, after she had managed to spring to her feet, Lily reached for the little one. The thundering tra-ta-ta-ta-a struck the child before her mother could shield her. The young child looked like a little angel with her cherubic mouth slightly open and her eyes turned towards heaven, only this angel was motionless. Lily's screams were quelled in an instant by other bullets which pierced her head and heart. Other babies were merely smashed against the stone wall by the raging madmen who decided to save their bullets.

All this we heard from the few mothers who escaped Plac Zgody alive. But were they alive? Could a mother really be alive after one or more of her infants was torn away from her breast and killed? We could only share in their wish that all through the days, nights, and dawns, the cries of those children and the eyes of those babies would glare at the barbarian stone men wherever they were.

Mojshele was now one of the few children left in the ghetto. Every time someone knocked at the door, Mother hid him in a closet. One day we came from work, and Mojshele was nowhere in sight.

"Mother, Mother," called Anna, "where is Mojshele?" My heart stopped beating. "My God," Mother sighed and rushed to the closet. When she opened the door, there was Mojshele in a little bundle, sleeping peacefully. Carefully, we took him out and carried him to bed.

"Mother, how could you?" Pola asked.

"Darling, I forgot all about him. First of all, after someone knocked at the door, I hid him quickly in the closet. It was Mrs. Zelmanowicz who came, and you know how she can talk. Well, she talked and talked until it got late and I had to fix some dinner, so, from one thing to the other, I forgot about the poor baby."

Before Easter, the Jewish bakery in the ghetto was allowed to bake the Passover bread, the matzos. Each family received a pound per head. On the eve of Passover, our family sat together at the festive-looking table, with candles flickering and our faces shining. Father chanted the Haggadah.

Mojshele, as the youngest in the family, asked: "Ma nishtana halaila hazeh?" (Why is this night different from all other nights?)

Father began: "For on all other nights we eat either matzo or bread, but tonight we eat only matzos." Before Father had a chance to finish the sentence, Pola burst out crying.

"The Jewish people have survived and Judaism will live no matter what the persecution. Don't you children lose your faith in God," Father pursued with conviction, looking at Pola.

"Amen," added Mother.

"For on all other nights we eat any vegetables, but tonight——"

Mojshele broke into tears.

"We can do without the bitter herbs, Father, it is bitter enough," Mania said.

Mojshele finished the four questions and Father went on reading the Haggadah. When Father raised the cup of wine, he recited: "It is God's promise that has stood by our fathers and us."

Listening attentively, I leaned forward because Father seemed to put more meaning than usual in his words. He spoke slowly and clearly:

"For it is not only one man who tried to destroy us, but in every generation there were those who tried to do so. Yet, the Holy and Blessed One always rescues us from their hands."

As he ceased to pray, Father reclined in his chair and looked forlornly at our faces. Tears glistened in our eyes, but we were not crying. Father continued with the Seder, passing the wine. To our surprise, Mother had brought forth a bottle of wine, which she had made from raisins. She had saved it all this time so each of us would be able to make kiddush on Passover.

Dinner followed. "A chicken!" Mojshele touched it with disbelief. I knew that Father had been trading Mother's jewelry for additional food. Mother still boiled a pot of soup every day and on Fridays she had a welcome piece of meat floating in it. But a whole chicken!

"That must have cost a diamond ring, Father!" I exclaimed.

"Never mind the ring. How do you like the chicken?" Mother asked. "You see, kinderloch, what did I tell you? As long as there is life, there is hope. Even a chicken on our table!"

The next day, for the second Seder, I was invited to Mark's family. I had seen Aron's friend many times since the day we had met at Sophia's. Each time he came to our house, he would be surrounded by all the girls. Pola was always after him to relate the latest news about the advances of the Germans; Anna watched carefully to see if he held my hand and how he looked at me. I, myself, listened to Mark, for he had an interesting way of telling stories.

Mark's family greeted me warmly that Passover night. His Mother served soup with matzo balls and a piece of cake for dessert. Far better than the food, however, was the festive mood which reigned at dinner. Mark's father chanted the Haggadah. Mark and his sister Bella responded.

After dinner Mark walked me home. He held my hand and every now and then twirled me around and looked into my eyes. When I began to say goodnight, he drew me to him and kissed me on the lips.

"Mark, Mark, I don't want you to do that," I protested.

"No, of course you don't. You think I can just be with you, look at you, and admire you. But to kiss you, oh no, that you don't want. Or maybe you are afraid? Ruth, can't you see? I love you! I love you more than anything in the world. I do."

"I love you," echoed in my ears as I rushed up the stairs. I stopped for a moment, pausing unsteadily. What did this mean?

I felt two opposing currents struggling within me. The one tugged: I desire Mark, I do want to kiss him and be held by him; but the other one, the stronger, more powerful one, overcame the first: I can't. War is the only present reality. I don't dare to get close to anybody or anything. It is quite mad. Tomorrow I might be separated and the pain will be unbearable. Above all, I can't form attachments to people, to things, to flowers, to birds; I can't look forward—not even in my dreams can I trust my feelings because tomorrow they will all perish and then emptiness, bitterness, misery.

15 Although we knew it was May, somehow we didn't feel it in the air. We couldn't see the quivering trees opening their buds, nor children playing in the streets. It was just another tedious month. However, in spite of the life-denying influences affecting us daily, in spite of every outward assault divesting us of our humanity, a strange atmosphere was developing in the ghetto. More keenly than ever, everyone could feel the vital need for love, for friendship, for solace. Everybody was clinging to somebody, trying to preserve something lasting and enduring, if only for a fleeting moment.

It was at this time that something quite out of the ordinary ignited our enthusiasm and helped us to forget about the war, our somber existence in the ghetto, and the constant lack of food. Remarkable as it was, the Ordnungsdienst (Jewish Police) received permission to put on a concert for the ghetto population. This meant that anyone living in the ghetto who was talented as a pianist, singer, or violinist was invited to perform. Needless to say, all through the week, we were overjoyed as we prepared for the gala evening.

"Who knows? The Germans must be losing the war, and they want to make up with the Jews," Mania speculated.

"It's a wonder the Germans want the Jews to be entertained. Why? And what for?" Father questioned.

"They want to gather us all together in one room," Pola said drearily, "and then they can do whatever they want — even burn us alive. That's the show they want to put on! I am not going. They won't see me burn alive." She pulled off the dress that Mania was sewing for her.

"Fine! Mania, you can finish mine instead. I wouldn't miss it for the world. Imagine, a concert in the ghetto! I can already hear the music playing." I began to move in dancing steps.

"Come on, Ruth, pretend I am Mark. Close your eyes, I am holding you in my arms and looking at you, like that, see? Now you can open your eyes, and don't step on my toes," Anna clowned.

Saturday evening, Mark called and walked Mania and me to the concert. Despite all the rumors and speculation, at least five hundred people from within the precincts of the ghetto entered the auditorium. I, too, felt suspicious at first, but when the concert started, I was caught up by the ever-varying strains of Beethoven, Bach, and Wagner.

What I felt was hard to describe. I floated in another world, an enchanting world. The part of me that lived in the dismal ghetto no longer existed. I felt released, uplifted. Throughout the concert, Mark and I exchanged tender glances. All these glimmerings of hope—the music, the singing—so elated me that I, too, wanted to sing, laugh, rejoice and cry, all at the same time.

Following the performance, the applause rang loud and long. Afterwards, the auditorium was filled with chattering about the magnificent soloists and the great composers. We could have been in any threater in the world. Abruptly, however, the happy noises died down as the crowd faced the SS guards standing around the hall on every side. Regardless of this, with the music in my heart, we walked by the guards, unafraid, and into the narrow, cobblestone streets, half-lit by the cloud-covered moon, towards home.

Before we entered my own doorway, Mark said, "I do hope we shall have some more concerts. It was a lovely evening, Ruth. May I kiss you, please?" I let him kiss me and rushed into the house, wanting to keep all the memories of this evening forever. But like all such rare occasions for joy in the ghetto, it was not meant to last.

The next morning, I slept late. We made every effort to sleep longer on Sundays so as not to hear our stomachs grumble, as there were hardly any rations left by the end of the week. However, this Sunday, a loud knock on the door roused me earlier than usual. It was Bella, Mark's sister, her eyes red and swollen.

"They took my father and Mark. They came at night for Mark. Because Father fought them, they took him, too. Nobody knows where," she cried hysterically.

By now, Father had awakened and was pacing the room. "Where is your mother?" I asked Bella.

"She is home, but she is going out of her mind. Please, Mr. Bachner, do something, please. They can't take my father away," Bella cried, pulling at Father.

"Bella, please, darling, I said, they must have taken them to work. They will be back." But my last words died in my throat, for the tears were choking me.

I dressed quickly. "Let's go to your mother; she needs you." Together, we ran to her house. The streets were deserted. I reached Mark's house, pushed open the door, and screamed. I fainted at the stark horror I saw before me. When I opened my eyes, Mark's mother had been placed on the bed after the neighbors had disentangled her from the sheet with which she had hanged herself. Bella was sobbing pitifully over her mother's body. Thoroughly bewildered, I sat at the table—the very same table where only a short time ago we had been singing, laughing, and rejoicing at the feast of Passover—the nightmare intermingling with the dream.

The passage I had read rang in my ears: "Thou redeemed us from Egypt, O Lord, Our God, and freed us from the house of bondage, and fed us in times of famine and plenty, saved us from sword and pestilence, and spared us from truly serious illness."

"Where are you now, great Lord, who cannot spare us from the Germans, the creatures of your creation?" I mused bitterly. With grief, I watched the men come one after another. They brought a wooden box, prepared the body, and removed it for burial. Later in the afternoon, I took Bella home with me, and she stayed with us, sharing our rations and our family's bed.

As the days went by, I missed Mark much more than I was willing to admit. Who can say how I would have felt had I parted from him under other circumstances? But all this was so different. For him to be taken out of the midst of life and love was extremely painful for me. I thought of all the ordinary things that any girl would have wished to tell him, such as the places I would have loved to have traveled to with him, providing we both survived the war.

"Litwo Ojczyzno Moja," Pola would sound off, every time she saw me deep in thought. I was beginning at last to understand Pola and her hero, Adam Mickiewicz. His philosophy began to make sense: "Litwo Ojczyzno moja Ty jesteś jak zdrowie, ile Cie cenić trzeba ten tylko sie dowie, kto Cie stracil." (Lithuania, my country, you are like health: one only learns how much he values you after he has lost you.) Truly, despite all our efforts, we really can't see the value of things, or people, until we lose them. And in my heart, I knew I had lost Mark forever.

16 We learned to worship work, for the Germans promised that as long as we worked we would live. Every few months, they developed a different system and issued another working card. Those who didn't receive a new card, as we later learned, were destined to be transported to Auschwitz where most of them died in the gas chambers.

During the night of 27 October, the ghetto was surrounded by German police. At first, the Jews were thrown into panic, many escaping through the canals and others finding a temporary shelter outside the ghetto. The Germans, however, lured them back with promises of work. Since the Polish population of Krakow wasn't at all anxious to hide them, they meekly returned only to be deported later.

The time of the week we dreaded most of all was Sunday. Especially on Sunday, with no rations left, we were always at home. It was then that the Germans would come and loot our dwellings. From whatever was left of our belongings, they initially took all the jewelry we possessed, then gradually our clothing and any other valuables. Quite often they robbed us of the few food rations we had.

Also, it was on Sundays that they executed anyone they had segregated, including the transports of men, women, and children. On one of these devestating days, towards the end of the winter, a commotion in the street wakened me. My father was already at the window. The SS guards were jabbing and prodding a group of young professional men with their guns, forcing them to enter the waiting trucks.

Father pointed to a young man in a raincoat among them who at that moment defiantly pushed the rifle away and climbed onto the truck. "He is the young doctor from the hospital who operated on your sister Anna when she had the bullet in her leg. Remember when you were walking from work and that young German just for sport was firing shots at both of you? We need a doctor here in the ghetto for our own people. What do they want of him, I wonder?" Father continued.

Pretty soon the two trucks loaded with the selected men left, and I hurried into the street for news. I came across an elderly woman kneeling on the sidewalk, calling in despair: "My son, my boy." Having helped the poor soul to her feet, I put my arm around her. But she continued raving: "He came home late; it was just before curfew. A minute later, we heard the knock on the door. Once I saw the Jüdisch Ordnungsdienst (Jewish Police), I knew something was wrong. A mother can feel," she said, her trembling hands pointing to her heart.

"He tried to give me courage. He kissed me, and then he was gone. I may never see him again," she sobbed.

"Please go home now, you should be there when he comes back." Leaning on me, muttering in her grief, she walked slowly towards her empty home.

Thereafter the Sunday transports became a ritual. Each time, a group of fifty or more men, women, or children were taken away in trucks, and nobody knew their destination. Everyone shrank in fear and held their breath not knowing what to expect, or who might be next. Frequently, I would run to Grandmother's to see if everybody was still at home. It always cheered her to see me, and she was grateful that her six sons who were brought into the ghetto were still safe and alive.

But one Sunday morning, her youngest son, my uncle Jerome, was taken away. This was the first tragedy that struck close to home. From then on, our life was bound to change. Grandfather prayed incessantly; Grandmother refused to talk to anyone for fear she might say something that would incriminate her or one of her children. We became afraid of each knock, a noise, or footstep.

In the quiet of the night, I could see the dim outlines of our sleeping family and hear their even breathing. It was Pola who many times screamed out in fear, tormented by nightmares.

By now, there was hardly any family in the ghetto who had not been touched by tragedy. In addition, the stocks of clothing and food in the ghetto stores were not steadily replenished. Hunger set in, and owing to the constant washing, our clothes wore out.

The limited free time we had from work, we spent together confined to our kitchen, which by now felt like a home. Mania mended our dresses, Pola diligently read her books, and Anna continued to tease us and talk a blue streak, while Mojshele whimpered and wanted to know how long the war would last and why couldn't we go back to our house and his own bed. Mother, always cheerful, had an answer for him: "The war won't last much longer, my son. It can't last much longer." Soon, we discovered that by no means was each peril that confronted us the final peril.

Disease was spreading through the ghetto. One Monday morning, I was feeling queasy. Pola always complained, "a blue Monday." In a way we were glad we had survived Sunday, but it was hard to get up on an empty stomach and go to work. This morning, I simply couldn't get up. My head felt heavy and ached.

When Mother touched my forehead, she decided that I was burning with a high fever and that I'd have to stay in bed. After everyone left for work, Mother arranged for a doctor to come.

He said he would come to see me soon, but he didn't arrive until late that afternoon. As badly as I felt, I couldn't help but laugh when I saw a short man in a long overcoat, reaching almost to the floor. Even worse, it looked like his mother's coat. His face was drawn, but his eyes were quick. He looked at me, took my temperature, and kept shaking his head.

I wished he would stop shaking his head; it made me dizzy. Terribly dizzy. I was turning around and around. I was dancing. I was twirling. The room was large and full of flowers. In the middle stood a big table, rising and falling, loaded with food. Loaves of bread, milk, and apples fluttered and swayed. Apples! How I wished to reach out for one! But a young man was holding me, dancing away from the table. He was holding me tightly. It was Mark. He bought all the flowers for me. "I love you," he kept saying. "Hold me, Mark, please hold me," I was begging. But his face became dim and slowly disappeared. Instead, the face of my mother was bent over me as she wiped the sweat from my forehead with a damp cloth.

"Feel any better?"

"I feel fine," I answered faintly, but my feet felt numb and my head very heavy. I closed my eyes.

The next morning the doctor came again. His verdict— typhus! After talking at length with Father, they decided that I had to go to the hospital for fear the whole family may become infected. Mother dressed me, and she and Father carried me to the hospital, which was not far from our house. In spite of feeling sick and miserable, I worried about Mojshele. Then I noticed he was at the door as I was leaving, throwing kisses to me.

The nights at the hospital were long and dreadful, the cries of the women ghastly. Some of the patients moaned, "Nurse, nurse, please help, water, water." Others raved from high fever. Every night the corpses were removed, and just as fast, the hospital filled with new patients.

In a few days, my fever went down and I felt fine. I had none of the symptoms the others suffered so terribly from. "Nurse, I can't be as sick as the others. All I have is a slight headache." But the nurse was too busy to answer. She came every morning, took my temperature, shoved the basin under me, and rapidly removed it. I called her Nurse Iceberg. She was the only nurse taking care of the seven women in my room, and on my third day there, two more beds were added.

The following morning I was guided to the laboratory for additional tests. After two days of quarantine, I was released, no typhus. Long into the night I sat together with my dear ones, praying and thanking God for this miracle. But I soon learned that my prayers were answered in more ways than one.

The Germans had discovered that typhus and typhoid fever were spreading in the ghetto. On Sunday, 14 March, 1943, a military attachment of SS men headed by the ghetto Commanders Get and Haas marched into the ghetto. At their command, two thousand people were assembled on Plac Zgody and the surrounding streets. Troops were sent into the hospital to select those who perhaps wouldn't recover soon enough to go to work, and another commando was sent to the hospital for communicable diseases; everyone including the nurses and doctors were shot to death. An additional seven hundred inhabitants of the ghetto were executed on Plac Zgody. Two thousand others were shipped to Auschwitz. An overpowering dread spread through the ghetto when the streets strewn with dead bodies and the walls covered with human blood were discovered the next morning.

At work, the next day, I did everything mechanically. I didn't touch any food; I didn't hear any voices. All those suffering creatures in the epidemic hospital came back to me one by one—all begging for a drop of water or a pill to ease their pain. Nurse Iceberg—efficient, devoted, hardworking. "Never let your feelings mix with your work," she used to say. She was an iceberg to do what she had to do and not break under that heavy load. Only the Germans could have broken an iceberg like that. With a machine gun, it was so easy.

Instead of going home that evening, I stopped at Grandmother's. I found a group of men covered with shawls, praying. These men knew that praying in a group was forbidden in the ghetto, but to them it was the only salvation. In prayer they found peace and solace, even if it meant death. I, too, tried to find solace in prayer that night; and when finally I trusted my soul and my heart to God, I slept peacefully.

17 Winter had dragged on forever so it seemed. Our second year in the ghetto of Krakow came to a close during March 1943. We felt that we could shake off the worst of sufferings—the bitter cold, the executions, the perpetual, gnawing hunger, even the fear—if only spring with its warmth and sunshine might bring some miracle.

But nearly all mornings presented the same strict pattern. Like an unending ritual, every morning, numb and depressed, we stood in rows waiting to be escorted to work. This particular morning, however, the air was colder and more biting than ever; and to our astonishment, the guards didn't show up.

"The war is over; the guards didn't come. We can go home!" Anna shouted. "You're crazy," Pola scoffed. However, a few minutes later the Jewish Police came, and we were told to go home.

"But what could have gone wrong, Father? The Germans are still at war," I said questioningly. "They need the guns we are making, they need the tools. Who else do they have to make them?"

"I know, I know what happened," Anna said excitedly. "The Germans have lost the war. We are free! Mojshele, the war is over; we shall now go back home to Zablocie!" she yelled, and danced around the room with Mojshele.

"Stop it, stop it, you idiots!" Pola came over to them, pulling them apart. "You are dreaming! Haven't you seen enough? The Germans are here to stay until all of us are wiped out, wiped out, do you hear!" Pola started to cry bitterly.

"Now, now, my child," Mother said, brushing the hair from Pola's high forehead. "How beautiful you are, my darling, but how bitter."

"Find some work now, children. I'll go out to see what I can find out," Father said, walking out. Then he added: "Help

74

Mother as much as you can, and help each other. I'll be back soon."

Not until noon did Father return. "Nobody seems to know what to expect. Here and there, I did hear rumors that we might have to go to a concentration camp," he said.

"Papa, you don't mean the camp where they take all the Jews and kill them together?"

"She means Auschwitz, Papa," Pola said sharply.

"But this camp you're talking about, Papa, it's not Auschwitz where we shall all go?" Anna pleaded.

"And why shouldn't it be Auschwitz; aren't we the same dirty Jews as the others who are being sent there day after day?" Pola added.

"Papa," Mojshele said, drawing as close as he could to Father, "will I have to go to a camp? Please, don't let them take me there, please, Papa."

"Listen, will you all stop this now!" Mother insisted. "Let's do something; let's clean. Yes, that's it. And maybe sing," she added.

"Anu Olim Artza, beshira uvzimra" (We go to our country with a poem and a song), I began, singing. But nobody followed me. No one, in fact, stirred. The room was quiet, dreadfully quiet. The heavy footsteps of marching soldiers resounded in the cobbled street, damp and slippery with the spring thaw.

From the window casement, we could see hundreds of people being herded together by dour-faced German guards. Some Jews were yelling, some weeping, while others were still coming out of their homes. Soon the sound of heavy steps at our door made our hearts lurch. When we opened the door, two stern Jewish policemen were standing there. "Sorry, Joseph, we have orders. Everyone has to go."

"Has to go? Where?" Father asked in disbelief.

"They say we all have to go to a camp not far from the city. Don't worry so much, Joseph. Pack what you can and come out to Limanowska Street," the policemen said and left.

We all moved around the room in chaos; everybody was in each other's way. Of course, Pola hunted for her books right away. "Does it mean that I may even miss this paradise?" she murmured, looking sadly at the large room, the oversized bed where all seven of us had slept together, the warm stove, and the bench where she had so often curled up to read.

"Listen, kinderloch," Father began. "From now on, we may all get separated. You are young and strong, remember. You must think only how to save yourself, how to get over the difficult times. Turn always towards life; struggle to live, for life has so much to offer you. Even if we perhaps become separated—I mean, Mother and I—remember, we shall meet again when all is over. We will all return to Zablocie and live happily ever after." He ended with a quivering smile and an involuntary sigh.

I shuddered as I looked towards Mojshele, half-hidden behind Mother and hanging tightly on to her skirt. He is so young! How will Father hide him in an open street and protect him now? I kissed the little fellow tenderly and helped to pack his things.

Mother handed each of us a pillow case in which we put some of our clothes. Finally, she divided all the food that remained: a slice of bread for each, a little sugar, and a few potatoes.

One by one, we left the room in silence. Before I closed the door, I looked around wistfully. How strange it was that this one room which had housed all of us for two years of confinement was so hard to leave. To be sure, it had been a home with walls to hide within, a bed to sleep on, a stove to keep us warm. And had we not thought, when we first saw it, how would we ever manage? Should I not now say that we can surmount any trial?

Once we had reached the pavement, Father repeated, "Try to stay together, girls, if you can." Then he and Mojshele were separated from us and ordered to join the men's lines. Father kissed Mother and all of us one by one. The din and confusion made the four of us and Mother press closer together.

Clusters of people were still coming, or being dragged, out of their quarters. Some, still in nightgowns, resembled apparitions. Each countenance—young and old, healthy or sick—reflected the painful surge within each heart. Many, bristling with loathing, refused to move and were practically kicked into their places. Nobody knew what was going on.

Methodically, the guards went back and forth through the rows of people, sorting, picking their victims—the old ones, then the young ones. The older ones were crowded into another street together with the sick, many who could scarcely crawl.

Our row, we quickly concluded, could be the death row for all we knew. We stood paralyzed when the SS men reached us and one rested his sharp eyes on Anna. She drew up her youthful body to appear taller and, unafraid, looked into his eyes. Oh, God, please don't let him take her away from us, I prayed. When the SS men stiffly passed our row, we all took a deep breath.

Then I noticed a group of young children, barely fifteen and under, being lined against the dark, stained walls of the ghetto. "Mother, what about Mojshele?" I asked. Mother lifted her eyes in prayer and didn't answer me. What I dreaded was that Mojshele might have to be separated from Father but didn't even allow myself to think about it. Then, unexpectedly out of nowhere, I was startled to see Emil running towards us. Where had he come from?

"So far, I've been placed with your father and Mojshele," he said, as if in answer to my worries about my brother. Still in shock, I saw him leave before I could say, Emil, please take care of yourself.

When the guards weren't in sight, we sat on our bundles and rested. We had been standing there for hours. By now, thousands of people were gathered in all the streets of the ghetto. Some were crying, some were screaming. Others, hollow-faced from hunger and thirst, stood mutely in the cold air. Wherever my eyes rested, I saw agony, unsurpassed by any I had seen before.

When we had first come into the ghetto, we still had some clothes, food, and above all, hope. We thought that the war would last only a little longer. Now, two years later, our clothes showed the wear and tear, our stomachs were shrunken and empty, and our hope . . . well, I still hadn't given up, and yet I couldn't imagine how we could last much longer.

The Germans, however, had a most interesting "solution" to our problems. Whenever our situation seemed impossible to bear, they found something that would surpass it, something to show us we were actually lucky being where we were, for it could be worse—much worse.

In Ciemna Street, the guards kept counting and recounting the rows of the sick, who were made to stand at attention while this was going on—the young ones, the old ones, anyone for that matter whom they wanted to include. As soon as they had finished, the guards pointed their guns towards them, and with a brief burst of gunfire across the walls of the ghetto, all were shot to death.

"Are we going to be next?" Anna asked while Mother prayed. Poor Anna, only fourteen, knew that the Germans usually killed children her age, but fortunately she was big for her age and always tried to stand erect, so she had managed to survive until now.

Gradually, the cries and screams subsided into a deadly hush. The SS guards surrounded what remained of the female occupants of the ghetto and motioned us towards the gate. With our bundles in hand, our throats dry, we looked at the murderers, dragging our feet with great effort.

18

We entered the city. The sun came through to greet us, but the air was very cold. The first line was formed by SS men pointing the guns, and the whole column was surrounded by many guards with machine guns. They were watching the prisoners—women and children who had never even stepped beyond their own homes, their families, whose only crime was that they had been born Jewish. But these people had the great strength to continue to live with their faith in the one and only God, and to follow the teachings of the Torah in spite of persecutions.

Is it possible that we shall survive this, too? I asked myself. Maybe, I thought, maybe now we have a chance to escape. After all, there were less than a hundred SS men surrounding us. Then I said: "Look, look, Pola. See all those people watching us from their windows?"

"Sure, why not, a circus has come to town," Pola grumbled.

"Can you imagine, if they all got together, they could take us away from the SS men easily," Anna echoed my thoughts.

"My, are you a dreamer! You never give up, do you? Can't you face it? The Poles will never help a Jew. Just look at them hiding behind the curtains, pretending not to see or hear. They must be happy we are leaving their precious town, even if we all get shot in the end. What do they care?"

"I have a plan," Mania whispered. "I'll push one SS man towards another, they will start fighting, and in the meantime all of you will escape. How about that?"

"Of course, you push him, and within seconds, the other one will shoot you. We then run away and try to hide in a Polish home; they kick us out and in a minute the Germans shoot all of us. What a beautiful ending to a struggle for survival in this war," said Pola sarcastically.

"I can't get over how you can always paint the darkest possible picture. I've told you over and over again that a miracle will save us all. I want you to believe in it," Mother said. We all trembled from cold and fear but marched slowly to the rhythm of the SS men's boots, waiting for the miracle.

The streets of Krakow were behind us now, and all we could see were the chimneys of the houses and the majestic Wawel Castle. It stood there high on the hill overlooking the Vistula River. I found it very hard to imagine that the Germans were sitting there now. Wawel was the pride and joy of the people of Krakow. It covered ages of Polish history. All the great kings and leaders of the country were buried there, from Kazimierz Wielki to Józef Pilsudski. I wondered if their ghosts were haunting the Germans. Very soon, Wawel Castle disappeared from view, too.

As we marched further and further from the city, cold air blew over the empty fields. Murmurs went through the column. What are they going to do with us? Where are they taking us? One woman's guess was as good as the next.

"Why don't they just get it over with?" one woman shouted.

"Why don't they shoot us right here?" another one asked.

"How long do we have to march to be killed at the end?"

The thought of being killed at the end of this road had crossed our minds but not for long. We made a point never to think depressing thoughts for too long. Pola had difficulty playing along with us, but we tried to distract her and help her out of her gloomy moods. Besides, Mother was always there with her quiet, sweet, voice, and a glimmer of hope, no matter how bad things looked. Meanwhile the sun had come out in all its glory. Far over the hills, we could see many buildings, their roofs shining.

"Mother, look, new houses; they look wonderful! Is it possible that this is the concentration camp they were talking about?" Anna asked.

"You see, what did I tell you? Father and Mojshele will come there, too, and all will be well," Mother said.

"I am sure they will bring all the men, too. We shall all find work and have lots of fresh air. I am not afraid anymore," Mania stated.

"It looks like the houses are spread far apart. Do you think they will let us go wherever we want?" Anna asked.

"Of course, you silly. How can they watch all around, and

besides, where would you go? We shall have our work, we will get our food, and we shall live happily ever after," Mania said.

"Will you stop all that nonsense!" Pola shouted. "Can't you see? Look, look well, or put your glasses on if you can't see. There are wires all around your precious houses. Maybe they are even electric wires. Wonderful mousetraps; you touch them and they catch, but for good. Can't you see?"

Suddenly we saw it all. No one uttered a word as we walked slowly past the wires and through the gate, which had just been opened to let us in.

19 We stood for hours being counted and recounted. The bundles we'd brought with us, our precious belongings, were becoming heavier and heavier. We couldn't put them down, for the ground was very muddy, and after several hours of carrying mine, I wished I hadn't taken anything out of my ghetto home. After all, we were going to have a new home here and would get everything we needed.

The sun had set on the Plaszow Concentration Camp when hungry, exhausted, resigned, we were sent finally to the barracks. The four of us were assigned to barrack Number 10; Mother was separated from us and sent to barrack Number 16.

We discovered very soon that our beautiful new houses were nothing but wooden shacks. They were long and narrow. On the outside walls all around inside the building were beds, three stories high, made of wooden boards covered with a few straws. In the middle of the building were more beds. Between the beds was a narrow walk, and at the front of the barrack stood an old-fashioned stove for which there was hardly ever enough wood.

We grabbed the second floor, believing that it was easier to get to than the third and had a little more light than the first. Four boards, one next to another, were to be our home from now on. We put our little bundles under our heads, shared the two blankets we had, and huddled together. In no time, the four of us were in a deep sleep.

A whistle and the buzzing noise of two hundred women sharing the room with us had awakened me. I couldn't quite figure out where I was at first, but the sight of my sisters next to me relaxed my fears.

"Didn't you hear the whistle? Up with you all. What do you think, you came to a hotel or something? Out! Out!" shouted a heavy woman who was in charge of the barrack.

"There will be no breakfast today. There was no time to prepare anything," she continued as we jumped off our bunks, straightened the clothes we had slept in, brushed our hair through with our fingers, and pushed through the narrow walks to get outside. Once outside we were told to go to the Appellplatz, which was the large field in the middle of the camp.

Our stomachs were cramped with hunger and cold, but who could pay attention to a mere stomach. Things were happening. People were pushing from all sides. Hundreds of thousands of people gathered in the Appellplatz. What were they all going to do? How could we all find work? Would we be able to stay together? Where was Mother? What had happened to Father, and what about Mojshele? How could he get through this hell?

Anna was holding onto me. "Pola, Mania, where are you?" We pushed and pushed together with the waves of people, and finally, through all kinds of maneuvering, the four of us stood together.

Mania spotted Mother. She ran out, she pulled Mother towards us. A Jewish policeman pulled her back. There were Jewish policemen and German policemen. There were men and women. The whips of the policemen reached far and wide—one could hardly hide. One whip almost hit Mother. Anna screamed, but by this time, Mother was standing in another row not far from us.

We were counted and recounted. Pushed in one direction and then another. We stood there for hours, hungry and tired. Finally, when the sun was about to go down, we were told to go to our barracks and report to work tomorrow morning.

From the Appellplatz, we rushed into the lavatories. Even though we hadn't had any food for two days, our bladders needed to be emptied. Thousands of women were pushing their way in. The lavatory was one long barrack. Against the walls were boards with small openings, almost too small to sit on. Very uncomfortable indeed. The Germans had a purpose and a plan for everything. You couldn't sit long, for the board would cut into your flesh. So one sat, one finished, and up one went! Everything was done mechanically and fast. At the end of the barrack were a few sinks with water dripping very slowly. There was nothing to dry one's hands with, but nobody bothered, for the water was too precious, and if one could get a few drops, one would drink it right out of one's hand.

Anna got off the toilet and held onto me. "We are going to work together, aren't we?" she kept repeating, as she pushed her way to the sink where she caught a few drops of water in her hand and drank it. Mania and Pola were somewhere in the crowd. Suddenly I saw them. They were pushing towards us with Mother. Mama, Mama, I missed you so," Anna cried and ran into Mother's arms.

"I just came from the men's barracks. I saw Father and Mojshele. They brought them to Plaszow, too. They brought all the men from the ghetto here. Imagine, Father saw Grandmother and Grandfather. They brought them to Plaszow too. They will work. I know they can do it. Oh, my God, I can't believe what is happening," Mother lamented.

"But what about Mojshele?" I asked.

"He didn't have to go to the Appellplatz this morning. The Jewish Police told him to stay inside the barrack. There are only about forty children his age in Plaszow. The Jewish Police are afraid the Germans won't let them stay in this camp. This is going to be strictly a working camp. Those who work eat. It's that simple. The Jewish Police are willing to hide the children as long as they can, and I think that as long as Mojshele is with Father, there is nothing to worry about. Your father will always find a way."

I could scarcely hear mother's last words, for the crowds were emerging from the lavoratories. The whistle blew, and we had to go to the barracks. There were many barracks in this camp. The men's barracks were to the east and women's barracks to the west of the Appelplatz. There were big barracks and smaller barracks. Ours was rather small, only two hundred women.

"Come and get it," the Blockälteste (woman in charge of this barrack) shouted. We rushed toward the front of the barrack where there was an iron stove. Standing on four legs with a long pipe leading to the outside and a lovely warm flicker of fire shining from inside, it looked majestic. If only I could feel like that for one split second. But I couldn't feel anything. Things were happening, orders were issued, and I as well as all the others followed mechanically. Just as now, we all rushed towards the Blockelteste who gave each of us a piece of bread and a tiny little square of margarine.

The women pushed one another, afraid there wouldn't be

enough for all of them. While we received bread, the others were getting a ladle of cold black coffee. We didn't want to drink it at first, but the woman in charge said: "You'd better drink whatever you can; otherwise, your guts will dry out."

We each swallowed the black water. When we went to our bunks, we decided that we should eat only three pieces of bread at night and in the morning we could divide the fourth into four little pieces. This way, we would have something in our stomachs in the morning, too.

Stella, Hanka, Sabina, and Henia, who had gone to school with me, were assigned to our barrack and took bunks next to ours. We were all young, strong, and anxious to talk and laugh or even reminisce, but when evening came, we were so confused, so overwhelmed with what was happening to us, that we didn't feel like talking. When the lights went out, we were all fast asleep.

When the whistle blew in the morning, I was awake. I put on my dress, which the night before I had taken off and folded carefully under my head. I knew now that whatever we had was all we had, and all we were going to have for some time to come. I had to take care of my clothes.

When Mania, Pola, and Anna were ready, we divided the slice of bread from the previous night's supper, rushed to the lavatories where we swallowed a few drops of water, and went quickly to the Appellplatz.

For hours, again and again, we were counted and recounted. Several guards surrounded a column of about five hundred women, and we were marched towards the southern part of the camp. This was where the work was done. Many barracks had been transformed into workshops and factories. Some of them manufactured army equipment, some uniforms, and some even paper and other materials necessary for German warfare. Here again the Jews were going to produce, to help the Germans fight the war against the Jews.

We passed many barracks and a large open area, and for a moment it seemed like we were going outside the camp. Unfortunately, we were stopped in front of a large group of barracks still within the barbed wire. We were told, however, that they belonged to a private enterprise called Madritch and that we were going to make uniforms for the German army. The men in charge, who were standing at the door, seemed pleasant, even human.

20 We were told that as long as we fulfilled our work quota, we would get enough food and some clothes. When we walked into the barracks, all I could see were sewing machines, hundreds of sewing machines, and green fabric all around. "What am I going to do? Why didn't I ever learn how to sew?" I moaned.

Mania looked at me and then pulled me towards a table where a group of older women were already seated. I couldn't understand why she made me sit down quickly, but I soon realized what was happening. On the table were ready-made uniforms and a box of buttons. Mania, with her sewing ability, had seen immediately that these must be the women who sewed on the buttons, and she knew that for that no training was required. I watched Mania, Pola, and little Anna sitting at the sewing machines; Mania sat in the middle. I could easily watch them from where I was seated.

"You want to sew on buttons?" a woman next to me asked. "Yes," I mumbled. "Here." She put a big bundle of uniforms on my lap. "We have to finish fifty each day; your little fingers will be pretty pricked by the end of the day."

I threaded a needle and started to sew on a button. The fabric was thick, and I knew the woman was right, but I also knew I had no choice, for more than anything else I had to be with my sisters. Mother and Father were also working together we had learned.

Mojshele was really something to worry about, but so far everything in Plaszow seemed good. And the man had said, if we did our work, we would have nothing to worry about; especially, here at Madritch, as it was still a private company working for the SS troops. What a delight it was when at noon the whistle sounded for a break and each of us got a bowl of hot soup, with big pieces of potatoes swimming in it!

"How are you doing?" Mania asked.

"Well, I don't know. I could never sew fifty jackets."

"Do as much as you can. They won't count."

"How about Anna? How is she going to finish her quota on the machine?" I asked.

"We shall manage. I can slip a few uniforms her way, and Pola can easily do it, too. I am so glad we are all together; I only hope Mojshele will be all right," Mania whispered to me as we were going back to the machines.

Hundreds of uniforms were finished at our table every day. I found it very difficult to complete my assignment, but pretty soon all the women around the table were helping me. They were thrilled to have a young girl among them. Each of them could easily have been my mother. The years of experience they had had in sewing enabled them to do it faster, and in no time, they completed my assignment for me. The thought of making uniforms for the Germans always bothered me though, and I wished that every button sewn on would strangle the SS man who was wearing it.

Each morning we waited patiently for our bowl of soup. When noon came, we all rushed outside planning neither to be first in line nor last but to be in just the right spot. Those at the beginning of the line would be served from the top of the pot, which was plain water; in the middle the soup was a bit thicker; but the next to the last part of the pot had all the ingredients of the soup.

Pola and Anna always managed to push their way around the middle. Mania stood near the end of the line; many times the soup ran out, and she was left with an empty bowl. Then we all shared ours with her.

"Danka, put the spoon in and reach for a potato," I said in a lowered voice to my friend who was spooning the soup from the pot. What a joy it was when she reached in and came out with a chunk of meat. But most of the time I came back with what looked and tasted like dirty water. It filled the stomach for a while, however, and when the workday was coming to an end and our stomachs rumbled, we would pretend that we were cooking and baking: "Do you know what my son likes best?" Mrs. B. began. "Pierogi! When I made pierogi, my son could eat as many as three dozen!"

"Mrs. B., let's make pierogi," I said.

"All right, pierogi it shall be. Take a handful of flour, do you have it? Good! Mix it with water and one egg, no more;

now, mix it well. Very well," she urged as I was going through the motions of kneading the dough. "now, take out a chunk of butter, a nice big one. Don't be stingy. Also, slice some onions into the frying pan. That's right. Make them nice and brown but not burned.

"I forget. Are we making the potato pierogi? Yes, good, because that is what my son likes best. You'd better boil some potatoes then. You do have some fresh boiled potatoes, but cold? Perfect! Mash them; put in a big spoonful of cottage cheese, then the onions with the butter and mix it well.

"Now," she continued, "roll the dough, make little squares with a knife like that, you see? You are a good cook. You are going to make a good wife for someone. Look how you learned to make pierogi. We are almost ready. Put the filling in each square, make it into a triangle, and close it. Now this is where the know-how comes in. If you don't close them well, all the insides will boil out. So you roll the ends with your little fingers, like that, and then throw them into a pot of boiling water. You see, all done! Then you watch them boil and in fifteen minutes you can take them out. You can't wait? You're hungry, oi vei!"

I could see her tongue rolling in her mouth just as mine was when I thought of tasting those delicious pierogis. While the other women were sewing buttons, I was serving the pierogis, and they all went through the motions of eating them.

Pola walked over just then. "How are you doing?" she asked.

"Want some pierogis? I just made some. Here," I answered.

"You and your crazy ideas. I would much rather have a slice of bread. I made the uniforms for Stella, and she is going to give me half of her portion. Her brother brings her more bread; he gets it somewhere. Well, I'd better be going; the stooge is watching. I hate him," she said in a low voice as she went back to her table.

The taste of pierogis disappeared from my tongue, but soon, someone else started to cook. Sometimes we cooked the most extravagant dishes. I would get so engrossed in it that I could feel the taste of the food on my tongue. Mrs. B. who was a short but heavy woman was very fond of me and decided there and then to teach me how to cook and bake all her recipes. She showed me a picture of her son, which she always carried tucked in her breast. "Look at my beautiful boy," she would say.

I looked at the picture of a young boy in a high-school uniform, his face hardly showing under his cap. I couldn't see anything beautiful about him, but I nodded my head. She told me that her son had been taken to Auschwitz, but that he would soon come back to her because he was her only son and she couldn't live without him. We all felt sorry for her and never interrupted her dreams; of course, we knew nobody ever came back from Auschwitz.

One day she told me how he was taken away in the middle of the night and how she had stood in the street all night and cried rather than go back up the steps to her empty quarters. I went over to her and put my arms around her, vividly remembering the dreadful night her adored son had been taken from her.

"I shall never forget your son," I told her. "I remember his face, and I can still see how they pushed him on that truck." But deep in my heart, I had the same feeling I'd had on that awful night: why does he have to die? He is so young and so handsome.

Mrs. B. wanted to sew all the buttons on for me while I simply sat and pretended I was sewing. Moreover, it seemed to give her pleasure when I told her stories about myself and my plans for the future. Sometimes she would bring a piece of bread that she had saved from the night before and would insist that I eat it. "The young need more," she would say, "and besides, I must take good care of you, so you can take care of my son." One day, she added "You are going to marry my son, aren't you?"

A few days later, she came to work, her eyes swollen from crying. She sewed faster than ever, but she didn't talk or even touch the soup we were given for lunch. "They sent his ashes, his ashes. My big beautiful boy in a little box. Ashes. That is all that's left of him," she moaned.

To be sure, she wasn't the first mother who had received the ashes of her child from Auschwitz. This was one more way of torturing people and taking away their hope. Sometimes it happened that by the time the parent received the ashes, the child was dead already; but several times the ashes had nothing to do with the real person. They were only sent to bring more suffering to the Jewish parents.

21 Every evening after work we had to report to the Appellplatz again. We were counted and recounted like precious jewels. When we finally entered our barrack tired and hungry, all we wanted was to go to sleep. One evening, I summoned all my strength and went over to Father's barrack to see Mojshele.

"Ruth, why don't you come to see me?" he asked sadly.

"Mojshele, my darling, how I wish you could always be with us. It is very difficult for me to come here. Many times we don't get back from work until just before curfew, and I can't let them catch me and put me in the dungeon. You wouldn't want that to happen to your sister. I miss you a lot, but it won't be long. Something is going to happen soon, and we shall all be together again," I said trying to cheer him up.

"You mean the war will be over, don't you? I won't have to hide under the bunk any more? You know there was an inspection in our barrack today. Our Blockalteste, you know him, he is nice; he hid me in the lavatory just before they came. He didn't want the SS men to find me here. He says I am too young for camp. Do you think I am too young? Maybe I could go to work? Ruth ..." he mumbled, and began to cry.

I took the little one in my arms. Father came rushing in. He kissed my forehead.

"How are you doing, Father?"

"Well, I go to work every day and hope to find you all here when I come back at night."

"Oh, Father, what are we going to do?"

"There is hardly anything we can do. I heard we are all going to wear uniforms, nice white and blue stripes. They think of everything. Now we won't be able to escape even if we tried to."

"Father, you can't mean it. What are you talking about? How can anyone even think of escaping with all the electric wires around and hundreds of SS guards all over the camp. Why, you would be shot before you could even take a step."

"I know all that, but I've got to do something with Mojshele," Father told me privately, walking away from Mojshele. "They are not going to let any children live in this camp; it is a work camp. You work; you eat, you live. You don't work; you don't eat, you don't live. I am losing my mind when I think what could happen. I must do something!" Father finished in desperation.

"Please, Father, it can't be that bad. I know you will find an answer. Don't worry, please. Something will come up; something has just got to." I kissed Father and hurried to kiss Mojshele goodnight because I had to return to my barrack before the whistle blew. As I walked back to my quarters, I, too, was worried, for I sensed that Father was truly frightened. Perhaps he knew more than he wanted to admit. I didn't say anything to my sisters that evening, but sleep wouldn't come all night.

It was May again. We could feel spring in the air and marched briskly from work to the barracks. One evening, when we reached our barrack, Mother and Father were waiting for us, their faces ashen. "They are going to ship all the children out of Plaszow," Father began.

"What do you mean, Father?" I looked at Anna and Pola. "No, I mean the little ones—Mojshele—the ones who are not working," Father added.

"Where are they taking them?" Pola asked.

"God knows," Mother answered. Her eyes were red from crying.

Father then explained: "They said that there is no room here for children; this is a work camp. They will probably send them to a children's camp."

"What they say and what they do are two different things," Pola snapped.

"What can we do? I knew this was coming, I knew it, and yet I was hoping, hoping for a miracle. Yes, the miracle your mother is always talking about. Nu, where is your miracle?" He turned to Mother.

"Why can't we hide him somewhere?" Anna asked.

"The Germans thought about that, too. Any child who is found in camp after Sunday will be shot to death. That is what they said."

"Imagine, the few children we have here in Plaszow; they don't do anybody any harm. They don't even get any rations. So they don't eat their precious bread or the cold soup. Why can't the Germans leave them alone?" Mania cried.

"Maybe this time they really mean what they say. Surely, this isn't a place for little children. Maybe this other camp has a school where they can learn and a place for them to live and grow up. Why do we always think the worst will happen? Why would they kill little innocent children? Did they cause the war? Do they have to fight it? Could they fight it with their little hands that can hardly hold a ball, or with the few words they have learned to say? No, I can't believe they would do anything to our children, Joseph," Mother concluded with a hopeful note.

"Well, if Mojshele hides here, he has no hope. But if he goes, like Mother says, he still has a chance," Anna surmised.

We all went to the barrack. Mojshele was waiting anxiously for Father. Skinny, frightened, his big eyes were enormous in his pale face. He ran to Mother and embraced her. For the next few minutes, we all kissed him and hugged him without a word. He had tears in his eyes.

I remembered again the day he was born, and father's words when we placed the golden coins in his first bath: "For he should live to be healthy and happy and rich." That night I was unable to sleep. I wanted my mother to comfort me, but knew she could no longer help any of us.

The following Sunday, the mothers brought their little ones to the Appellplatz.

"Mojshele, my dearest one, it is only going to be for a short time. We shall soon be together again. Take good care of yourself, please, my dear, my angel," Mother whispered.

"Rachele, my little one, this will be the last time we shall separate," another mother whispered.

"Bubele, my son, you must be strong, won't you?"

"Hannah, my dearest, you take care of your little brother. Hold him; he is so tiny."

"And remember, we shall all be together soon," the mothers repeated one after another. They didn't even cry, for they didn't want the little ones to see their tears. They smiled, gave them hope, and their hearts broke as they helped their children climb into the truck that was taking them away. The children huddled close to each other, cold and frightened.

22 The summer of 1943 was unbearably hot and sticky. More and more people were being brought from different camps surrounding Krakow as well as from small towns where ghettos were being liquidated. Often, people were brought in who had been found hiding in Polish homes, but we never saw them; we could only hear the sound of gunfire now and then.

When new people arrived, we rushed to their barracks, anxious for news, but they were unable to tell us what was happening. Rumors circulated that the Germans were losing the war, that the Russians were moving forward, that America had joined the western countries against the Germans and the Russians. There were all kinds of rumors, but we only listened and wondered whether anything would happen before it was too late for those of us in Plaszow Concentration Camp.

As transports came in, others were going out. Destination: Auschwitz. A few people went out of Plaszow into other working camps, but mostly, they were sent to Auschwitz. Eventually, however, this stopped, too. The Germans in Plaszow wanted to have their own show.

My uncle David, young and handsome, went to work one day with his two sons. He was told to finish a certain job by the end of the day. It was, of course, an impossible task. When five o'clock came, the guard entered: "You, Jew, you didn't finish your job. Sabotage!" And with this, the guard shot my uncle to death as his two sons looked on. The boys did not even have time to scream. They could only stand paralyzed at the sight of their father, lying dead in a pool of blood.

One Sunday morning, we were summoned to the Appellplatz. This was an unusual call, and we didn't know what to expect. We lined up in fives according to working groups as we did every morning and every evening, and waited. The number of SS men watching us was greater than usual, and the Jewish policemen, in particular, had a gloomy look. We noticed something that looked like a gallows in the middle of the Appellplatz.

"Why would the Germans go to the trouble of hanging people when they can shoot them instantly?" someone asked.

"They must add some color to the killing," Pola snapped.

Three young people, a girl and two boys, were brought in front of the gallows. A stillness, terrible, frightening, covered the Appellplatz. No one moved; even the guards and the Jewish policemen were motionless.

I didn't want to look up. I could scarcely breathe the air was so heavy. In spite of myself, my eyes rested on the girl. It was Hela, a school friend of mine. She seemed taller than she was, for she was so slender, and there was a haunting beauty in her large, clear eyes. She was self-controlled as she stood there in front of the gallows. The voice of the Commander shouted:

"These three tried to escape from work; they are charged with treason and sabotage! For this, they will hang!"

As the guard finished, the hangman tied ropes around the necks of the three and pulled up. My friend fell. A hissing sound went through the crowd. My heart was beating fast. Maybe they would let her live. I remembered reading somewhere that there was such a law: if someone was hanged and fell, he would be allowed to live.

For the Germans, however, there were no laws. Again, the noose was placed around Hela's neck, and this time there was no fumbling. We all had to watch. The guards were walking around our columns and making us look. Those who looked away were pushed with the guns; those who fainted, and many did, were poked with guns until they came to. I stood there and watched, trying to imagine that it was just another nightmare that would soon be forgotten.

We were slowly learning to live with horror, tragedy, and cruelty. We were becoming immune to it, or so we thought. Not long after the first hanging, we were called to the Appellplatz again on a Sunday. This time we knew we had to witness another spectacle the Germans had prepared for us.

I was in barrack Number 2, sitting and talking with my grandmother, when the Blockalteste came in. Grandmother was young looking and still able to work, and, fortunately, she had survived all the hardships until now. When the call came to go to the Appellplatz, she said to me: "I can't go this time. I shall stay in the barrack."

"But, Grandmother, you know what they will do to you if they find you here," I pleaded.

"My child, it doesn't matter any more. A few weeks ago, they shot my son. Today they may hang one of my other children. I can't be a witness to it any more." When I looked at her, her face had changed. She lay motionless on her bunk.

"Grandmother, Grandmother, what is it?" I implored. Her eyes were open, but she didn't see me. I ran to the camp hospital, pushing through the crowds, knowing that I must get a doctor and get back to the Appellplatz in time. My dear Grandmother. How much I had always admired her. How much I had learned from her. She was a generous, sweet woman, who had devoted most of her life to others. Outside of bringing up her own nine children, she was always ready when others needed help. If a girl couldn't afford to have a proper wedding, my grandmother would see to it that she had one. She would help young couples with their babies. She had her visiting days in the hospitals, going from ward to ward, bringing food or a nightgown to a new mother, or a bunch of flowers to brighten the sickroom.

We never knew where she was spending her time. In the evenings, she would tell us stories; little did we know that they were her own. In the last few years, she had lost many children and grandchildren. By the time I returned with a doctor, her eyes had closed forever. Death had come very quickly.

We all had to go to see another hanging and she stayed in her bed—her wish came true. Later that night, my father and his brother Herman carried her behind the barracks and buried her secretly on the grounds of Plaszow. Grandfather said a silent prayer for his dear wife and companion. Day by day, we were parted from our loved ones, and we wondered which of us was to be next.

The fear, the agony, and the pressure under which we lived was too much for me. I suffered unbearable headaches. I couldn't go to work, yet I knew that to stay in the barrack was dangerous. I went again to the camp hospital, and one of the doctors suggested that I be put under observation.

The hospital was a long, wooden shack, and Jewish doctors with very little in the way of medicines were allowed to perform simple treatments for simple illnesses. The hospital was kept antiseptic, the sheets were clean and the beds neatly made, at least. To my amazement, I received enough food to sustain me, and more. When Mother came to see me, I shared my soup with her. I even managed to save a little sugar as a treat for my sisters.

Six patients shared one room. Every morning the doctor came in, checked our pulse, our temperature, and cheered us up. My headaches were still unbearable. Zosia was in the bed next to mine. She was about nineteen years old. The hospital gown was hanging from her; there was nothing left but bones. She didn't know what was wrong with her, but she hadn't been able to digest any food for weeks. She had long, brown hair and beautiful, sad, brown eyes. When she got out of bed for a moment she was so weak that Dora, the girl in the other bed, had to quickly help her to get back in. Dora was strong and didn't look sick; actually, she was rather fat.

In the evening the hospital was deadly quiet.

"Ruth, are you awake?" Dora was standing next to my bed.

"I am going to have a baby," she whispered.

I jumped up.

"What did you say? Did I hear you right? Have a baby, here in Plaszow? Oh God!" I exclaimed.

"Dolek is so happy. I told him today. The war will be over soon and we shall have this baby. I only have five more months to go. The war will be over by then, don't you think so, Ruth?"

"Yes, of course." I put my arms around her and held her for a moment.

"Ruth, do you know what is wrong with Zosia?" Dora asked pointing to the next bed. "She is so sick. What are they going to do with her?"

"What do you mean, what are they going to do with her? Nobody is going to do anything. Can't you see how they are trying to help her? The doctor has been spending a lot of time with her, and she is a good doctor, I know. She will get Zosia out of it, whatever she is suffering from."

"I sure hope so," Dora whispered. Then she continued:

"Ruth, your hair is so lovely, so silky and blond, I hope my baby's hair is like yours. I hope it's a girl," Dora said dreamily, and walked back to her bed.

"Goodnight, Dora, sleep well," I whispered, and I knew that Dora would sleep well and dream about her little girl with long, silky, blond hair.

In the morning a nurse came in and told us:

"They are coming to inspect the hospital."

"What do you mean inspect? What will they do?" we asked.

"I don't know. They never came to the hospital before. They probably want to make sure that we are taking good care of you. Make yourself beautiful," she said.

We straightened our beds. Dora went over to Zosia and brushed her hair. She rubbed her cheeks to make them look pink, for they were alabaster-white. We all tried to make our faces red, and we brushed our hair, for we wanted to look healthy.

We heard the familiar sound, the marching boots of the SS men. Several SS men walked into the room. My heart stopped beating. They looked around, and within seconds, one pointed his finger at Zosia and then Dora. I was paralyzed. I was expecting his finger to point at me. In my mind, I wished I could pray, but my heart refused. For that split of a second, my heart gave up, I gave up. I was sure I would be next. The SS men turned away and walked out of the room. I knew life must have run out of my body during those critical moments, and yet I was alive.

Within minutes, the two girls were taken out of the hospital room to join many others who were already being loaded onto a truck. Another truckload of human cargo, another shipment. We all knew by now that the destination of these shipments was the gas chambers of Auschwitz, but how could we believe it? At first they put us in the hospital, they take care of us, and for what? Why? Why would they take a girl like Dora, a young girl, whose husband adored her, and who was going to give him a baby, why in the world would they want to kill her?

Once more, the hospital was dead silent.

The next morning I signed myself out and went to work in spite of my excruciating headaches. My friends were glad to see me back at work and alive, but my heart and my mind were with Dora and Zosia and all the unfortunate people who had been loaded on the trucks and taken away. I could hardly do my work, and the other women filled the assignment for me. More uniforms, more buttons.

My future "mother-in-law" as she called herself had cheered me up and promised that her son, the doctor, would cure me of my headaches. She was all alone now for her husband had been shipped out with a group of older people. Another cargo of human beings shipped to Auschwitz. She also expected to be shipped any day, but wasn't worried about it at all, for she believed that her son was in Auschwitz and would save her. Watching this woman work and even smile at me sometimes, and hearing her talk about her son, and how the war would be over soon, made me believe in it, too, and helped me to keep my faith.

I returned to the barracks in the evening, and mother cried, holding me in her arms. She believed that nothing could happen to us any more, for I was saved again from a certain death. Before we went to sleep that night my sisters and I speculated on what was happening outside our world. As Plaszow was located far from the city and surrounded by barbed wire, we couldn't see or hear what was happening in Krakow.

Was the city alive? Were there any people there besides us? Had the world come to an end? Isn't there anyone who is at least interested in what is happening to us? Doesn't anybody want to help us?

Are the Germans winning or losing the war? Was America in the war?

We had learned more and more about America in the last few years before the war, and we couldn't imagine that such a powerful country wouldn't be in the war. Wasn't anyone going to come and save us, or was the whole civilized world just going on living as before and waiting until we should all be slaughtered? Didn't anybody care? We were talking, we were hoping, we were guessing, for we didn't know anything except that every day our lives were more in danger. Every day we were weaker, more hungry, and more despairing.

In the morning we gathered in the lavatories, trying to catch a little of the water that dripped slowly through the faucets. We drank a little, washed our hands; and with what was left, we washed our underwear, for we each had only one set to wear.

With the rations getting smaller and worse every day, and our clothes worn and torn, we knew we couldn't last much longer. Moreover, we soon were able to detect whether the Germans had had a victory or a defeat. Many times we wished it were a victory because according to our estimates whenever they suffered a loss, we suffered more. What easier way to exact revenge for a defeat than to inflict pain on helpless individuals locked in a concentration camp? Every time the Germans were defeated, they would order a segregation in our camp and send a large transport to the gas chambers in Auschwitz. Quite often they wouldn't even bother with that; they would take a group of people outside of Plaszow and shoot them, after they had been made to dig their own graves.

Thousands of people were shot and buried on the grounds of Plaszow Concentration Camp. Who would be chosen to live and who to die was impossible to predict. The procedures didn't make sense any more. Those who were alive had a difficult time believing that it was their friends and their dear ones who were being killed before them, and that they were still alive if only for a little while longer. The fear was gone and numbness had taken over.

We lived for each day. For us there was no tomorrow.

23 There were hundreds of young girls and boys in Plaszow for whom life had just begun. They had been graduated from high school just before the war and were eager to go into the wide world, to discover it and to learn life's secrets. Then the war started, and their young world trembled. What was happening now was strange to them. They had never heard of such events in history; it didn't even happen in a book. Where could people get such ideas? They wondered how one human being could treat another with such cruelty? Was the world coming to an end?

Could it be that a young boy would not be able to kiss his sweetheart? Take her for a walk in the park, or to dinner, or a dance? Had it all been forbidden forever? Would these young women, like myself and my sisters who were just developing into womanhood, never be allowed to stay in their lovers' arms? Would they never have children?

Was this world going to end? Many times we wished it would. We wished the earth would open and swallow us all. The moments of despair were so overwhelming that one had to reach with all her might for something to hold on to, for hope, for strength, for sanity. We could see many young girls who had given in to despair; they walked in a daze, they swallowed the little food that was given to them, they moved, but they didn't live. Their bodies and minds deteriorated and in no time they ended in a mass grave outside of Plaszow. The line between life and death was extremely thin, and one could only cross it with a determination to live, to survive, with the inner power drawn by some from love or the tremendous power of faith and infinite prayer. Wherever this power came from, it helped many to survive and to take from life whatever there was left to take. Each and every day brought something new, and the strong belief that this something new could one day be good news kept people hoping, waiting, living.

I noticed that several girls from our barracks didn't return to their bunks at night. I was unaware at first of what was happening but soon learned the facts. The girls would get into the boys' barracks before curfew. They would hide in their beds, mostly on the third floor, where only their immediate neighbors could see them. There they spent the night in their lovers' arms, pretending no one could see them or hear them.

These girls believed that they would rather die after experiencing a love affair than not knowing what it was all about. A very special group were the selected "beauties" in the camp. They were to entertain the Jewish policemen. They managed to find an open barrack at night, one that was used as a workshop during the day, and without shame or sorrow, the girls performed what was expected of them regardless of who the men were. For this, they received a slice of bread or a little sugar. Among them were a few of my school friends, and I often asked them what joy they found in their orgies? Their answer, always the same, startled me: "I don't want to die a virgin."

"If you knew what fun we have, you would do the same; anyhow, what difference does it make what we do as long as we get extra food?"

Sometimes I, too, wondered what it would be like to spend a night with a man, if nothing else, to be in his arms, to be kissed, loved, cuddled. Just thinking about it made me feel warm, but I knew somehow, I could never do it, not here in the concentration camp. This wasn't a real world, and I was going to experience real love. I was going to wait for it to come my way.

Most of these girls became promiscuous; the rations were getting meager, and some of them couldn't withstand the hunger. We made up a song about the girls and every time one of them would pass, we would sing: "Za zupkę, za zupkę, i za kawalek chleba, dziewczęta dadza wszystko co trzeba i nie trzeba . . ." (For a soup, for a soup and a slice of bread, the girls will give everything, what they should and shouldn't . . .)

These girls were giving away what every one of them had dreamed of offering only as a gift of love. But the despair that followed, the hardness that came to their eyes made me wonder if it was worth it?

24 The sun was shining again. This was the spring of 1944 at Plaszow. Having Mother and Father around and being together with my sisters, keeping warm at night, and giving each other courage, we had survived the winter.

We were on our way to the barracks one Friday evening when I was aware of someone following us. I heard my name, turned back, and blushed. My cousin Emil, who until now had not shown a sign of recognition since we had entered the camp, came over to me and asked if I would come to see him on Saturday afternoon. He would be in his quarters.

He was wearing his shiny uniform and looked quite handsome, as I always thought, when I saw him from afar. He was part of the Ordnungsdienst, the Jewish Police. I had watched his transformation from a nice, decent young boy into a cruel beast possessed by power. I was ashamed to admit that he was my cousin when I saw his whip swinging through our rows on the Appellplatz. I often wondered whether it was his desire to be stronger than others or the bitterness of youth lost, of family life disrupted, that had caused this tremendous change in him.

When he asked me to see him, I tried for a while to forget what he was doing now and what I thought of him. As a policeman, he was a different person. Memories of times spent together long ago, wonderful, carefree days would come back to me; the days, when as little children, we had spent the summers together at Grandmother's. We would milk the cows early in the morning, take them out to pasture, run through the fields, and frolic and sing. As we grew older, we would climb the mountains surrounding Grandmother's farm—Romanka, Pilsko. We picked the little edelweiss and thought that just as these flowers, we, too, should live forever. Those were the real days. Today, nothing was real, nothing was beautiful.

I was glad Emil wanted to talk to me and see me even though I was puzzled as to why, after all this time. Perhaps he wants to go to bed with me, I thought. I was sure I was the only girl in Plaszow he hadn't slept with. He was young, he was handsome, and he was an Ordnungsdienst. He could have any girl he wanted. I was something different; I was a challenge to him.

When I walked into his room, he was resting, stretched out on his bed. He greeted me, his face pale and hard. "I am glad you came; I must talk to you," he said as he pulled out a chair for me and reached for some fruit, the sight of which amazed me because I hadn't seen any for at least a year.

He had witnessed a mass shooting the day before, he said, and among the victims was Fela. Fela had been Emil's girlfriend, but when we all went to the ghetto, she had stayed behind in hiding. Later, she met a Polish boy whom she married and lived with in a small village outside of Krakow. The Germans caught up with her, nevertheless. Their dogs must have smelled Jewishness in her; they always had a way. They brought her to Plaszow; she was expecting a baby any day.

"She looked at me," Emil said. "I wanted to die with her. I couldn't help her. I couldn't do anything. I was almost glad the first bullet killed her and her unborn baby, for I couldn't look into her eyes again. Shot to death with hundreds of others that they found hiding among the Poles. What's the use?" he suddenly cried out. "I can't go through something like that again, I can't," he continued. "How can any human being commit such a crime—killing a young, innocent girl with a baby in her womb? And I thought I had become immune to feelings!"

"I guess we all think we are becoming immune, and yet we still can't face it," I said.

"I stood there and felt like shouting, like getting back at them with my fists, with all my body, and yet when I thought what harm this could do to my family, I didn't even move. Or perhaps I was just afraid for myself. I didn't want to die. Can you understand that?" he shouted and shook me. "I knew you would understand, and I just had to talk to someone," he continued.

"What can I do? I was pushed into being a policeman by my family and was hoping that in some way I might be able to help them. Now I can see I have done more harm than good. I can't stand in front of all these helpless people and give orders any more. I cannot follow the Camp Commander's orders or take part in the orgies that go on all the time. Young innocent girls who never before would even think of doing something immoral are entertaining the Jewish police force, and sometimes they are supplied for the German commanders. This is crime . . . beyond crime," he stammered. All the illusions of love and youth were so terribly smothered for him. He didn't know what was right or wrong, real or unreal any more.

Suddenly he took me in his arms and kissed me passionately. "You are the only real thing in this world. Will you marry me?" he almost shouted. I was so stunned, I could scarcely breathe. This I hadn't expected, and I don't think he had either. It just came spontaneously. In his moment of grief and sorrow, he had felt an urgent need for someone to love him, to be near him. I knew he had always been fond of me, and I, too, had a great affection for him.

Once more he took me in his arms and kissed me, this time, tenderly, lovingly. For a moment, we forgot the world around us. I lay on his bed and he caressed my hair, my face, and looked at me with love. If this could last forever, how happy we would be, I thought. Then I quickly came back to reality. I knew I had to leave so that I could think clearly about all that had happened. I didn't want to hurt him any more, and after I told him I would think it over and let him know, I left his room, taking only a few apples to share with my sisters.

How could I possibly marry him, I asked myself, on my way back to the barracks? How could our marriage help him to escape from this dreadful present? How could he change so suddenly? What could I do to help him or change his situation? I knew then that I couldn't do it. Our marriage would only mean sharing his bed.

I went to see Mother and told her all about it. She had that wonderful smile on her face; she hugged me and kissed me, listened to me attentively. "The decision must be yours, my dear," she said. "If you think you will love him and want to marry him, then you must. You know, your father and I were cousins, too, but you must decide for yourself," she concluded.

When I lay on my bunk that night, I thought: here was a great temptation. I could live in a separate room, with just Emil and not with two hundred other women. I could get better food and many other privileges. I could have his love and somebody to look after me and take care of me. I knew Emil could ask any girl; and every one of them would say yes, even here in camp. Most of the girls lived from day to day, anyway, and didn't worry about the future. But I still had hopes and was looking ahead. I was looking ahead to the day when the gates would open and I would walk out into the new world with my head high and my conscience clear. I never went back to Emil's quarters. I avoided him and he must have understood why.

25 During the summer of 1944, the inhabitants of our concentration camp were in a demoralized state. Diseased physically and morally, the people were slowly giving up hope and the struggle to survive. Many workshops were closed. New transports were coming in, and segregations were being made day by day.

Every morning as we came to the Appellplatz, we wondered whether we would see our loved ones again. Since Mojshele had been taken away, Father had aged rapidly. His hair was gray and his face drawn and pale. The constant worry about Mother and us kept him awake at night, and during the day he had to work very hard in the paper mill on as little as one bowl of soup a day. Food was getting more scarce and worse all the time. I was heartbroken whenever I looked at my handsome father, who only a short time ago could have been mistaken for my brother. He was about forty-five years old but looked like an old man, and the danger of having him taken away was increasing. During the night, the barracks were raided and anybody with a sign of gray hair was removed. In the morning when people from all the barracks met at the Appellplatz, and later at work, they would learn who had been taken during the night. They knew that they would never see them again. Yet, the tears wouldn't come even then. We couldn't cry anymore. Many times I wondered what would happen if suddenly this mass of people were liberated. I thought what a different world it would be. This would have to be a different world from the one I had known before.

A world consisting of mothers whose children had been torn away from their breasts and shot or killed in front of them. A world where there were no children, no future generations. No little ones whose cries and laughter would fill the lives of married couples. Where growing children would have no mother or father to guide them and help them to grow. No parents to witness their weddings or cuddle their grandchildren. This would have to be a world without grandparents. A world where wives would live alone because their husbands were killed, or a husband forever mourning because his wife had died in the gas chamber. Where sisters were missing their brothers, and the brothers forever looking for their big or little sisters who they thought might have survived. A world where food would be the most important part of a human life, where warmth and a roof overhead would be the greatest luxury. This would have to be a world without laughter—a world of the dead!

Was such a world what we were suffering to live for? I wondered many times, and for days, each day I would go to work, work all day, and march back to the barracks with my head down, feet moving automatically, without the slightest desire to survive. But when I was in the barrack again with Mania, Anna, and Pola, and Mother or Father walked in smiling, seeing we were alive and in spite of everything growing to womanhood, my spirits would lift. After all, we were together, and we were well. We always remembered each other's birthdays, and on such occasions, nobody would touch their food rations. They were given as a birthday present.

When my birthday came around, I was given a real feast in the workshop. My sisters collected their rations, and my "future mother-in-law" baked something for me, although how she managed it, I would never know. It was a cake made from bread and potatoes, and it even had pieces of apple and some sugar. I was thrilled with my gift, but I felt guilty about indulging in such luxury, knowing that this must have cost her many a ration; but she was so glad to make me happy.

"After all, I must take care of my daughter-in-law, to preserve her for my son," she said to the others.

"She makes me sick talking like that," another woman said to me at the table, when Mrs. B. didn't hear. "How can she insist that he is alive and still wants you to marry him when she knows damn well that his ashes came from Auschwitz, and besides it is clear now that nobody gets out of Auschwitz," she continued.

I felt sorry for Mrs. B., but I always agreed with her that her son was alive. Since she lost her husband, her son was the only hope, and besides I enjoyed being treated as a daughter-in-law. By now I knew everything there was to know about her son. I knew about his boyhood and even about his girlfriends. I knew his habits, likes and dislikes. He was becoming someone close to me; he was real even though I didn't know him. I was sure that he had been killed in the gas chambers; I had seen his ashes. But deep in my heart, I was hoping that I might meet him one day, if only to tell him of his mother's love and devotion.

26 The end of the world had come, or so it seemed, at Plaszow on 6 September 1944. "Everyone report to the Appellplatz!" the Jewish policemen shouted, racing through the barracks.

They went into the hospital, their whips chasing every wretched soul out of their beds; those who could walk and those who couldn't. The will to survive the war helped even the crippled walk to the Appellplatz, for if they remained in bed, they knew they would be shot to death immediately. But in the Appellplatz, it was different. If they could stand erect for a few minutes, —in a sort of stoic resignation—possibly, possibly they could still be saved. Inevitably, this little thread of hope always worked miracles. Though an apparent impossibility, the crippled, the sick, and the half-dead somehow staggered to the Appellplatz, their lungs expanding for breath, their feet stumbling toward freedom.

"The Germans have lost the war," someone shouted reassuringly.

"They are going to finish us all," another one added with pathetic emphasis.

"They are going to let us all go free," Anna whispered. "Don't you think so, Ruth?" she continued. In my uneasiness, I didn't answer her. I was bewildered myself. There was a strange feeling among those in the Appellplatz. At first, there was a great rush to get into rows, then a considerable stir of whispering and guessing. Now we just stood in place as we had so often, being counted and recounted, without a drop of water, without food, hour after hour, while the hot September sun shone mercilessly upon us. As was usually the case, the longer we stood the heavier our hearts became. There was doom in the air. We could hardly breathe.

The SS guards were raging like wild beasts, giving orders and using their guns whenever someone fainted or was unable to stand at attention. The Jewish policemen watched, unable to help even their own families, whom they had been able to protect up until now. For these men, the uniform was the only way to help their families with a little more food, better quarters in camp; sometimes they were able to hide them in their own quarters when special calls came. But something like this was different. This call had been kept secret, even from them, and they were more or less all involved. Truly, the end of the world had come!

The four of us had managed to stay together, and we were able to get Mother into our row of five. Rows of men were being formed on the other side of the Appellplatz, but we had no idea where Father was. During the noon hour, we heard a rumor that a number of trains had pulled into the camp the night before. This brought on speculation and hopes that we would be shipped somewhere into Germany for work.

"Don't worry, my little angels," Mother said to us. "Once we leave the gates of this hell, we shall be free."

"The whole train will be saved by the Americans, and we shall be free," Anna echoed.

"Listen to this one; she sounds like something from another world," a woman in back of us said angrily.

"Mrs. Landau, my dear woman, don't you have any hope at all? You have survived so far, haven't you? You can take anything, I know," Mother answered, her own face drawn with suffering.

"I can take anything, you say? How can I, without water, without food? Look at me. Look at me. Mrs. Leon Landau, a human rag. My husband, the honorable Mr. Landau, was taken to Auschwitz long ago. He was the intelligentsia; he was one of the first to go. Then my little Rachele. She was only ten years old. She went with your Mojshele. Why did they have to take her away from me? How can she live without her mother? And you tell me I ought to have hope? Before the day is over, and I mean today, we shall all be finished right here on this Appelplatz. If only they would get it over with. What are they waiting for? Do we have to lose our minds, before we lose our lives? How much more can we take?" Mrs. Landau started to scream hysterically. An SS man was coming her way, and we tried to quiet her down.

"Mrs. Landau, don't you know we are going to Auschwitz? You will see your husband and Rachele," I said, completely unaware of what I was saying. The words just came out; I couldn't suppress them. The thought of Auschwitz had never crossed my mind, but there it was, and it sounded real. I knew instantly that this was our destination. My own words confounded me!

The sun went down, and a cool breeze moved with us as we were ordered to march towards the trains. Hungry, tired, parched from the sun, we came to a place where endless lines of freight trains were stationed. Should we climb aboard, or should we try to resist? It was impossible to grasp, let alone digest, the terrible scene. Nobody knew if death awaited us where we were going or if we were to be killed if we stayed? In the ebbing bustle, nobody knew, and finally seized with dread, nobody cared. Pushed by the crowd, the five of us finally found ourselves inside one of the freight cars.

Outside, people were still calling to each other, crying, running from one freight car to another, looking for members of their family. Nerves had reached the breaking point. Many people were falling, and others were climbing on top of them, frantically trying to get into the trains. From inside the car, I noticed that some women were pulling away—almost recoiling—from the trains. They were resisting, pushing, trying to stay outside, a poor little trickle of humanity groping for what even they did not know. For a moment, I, too, thought that we should escape from the train and remain in Plaszow to wait for whatever happened, but realizing that we were all together, I huddled in the corner with Mother, Anna, Mania, and Pola next to me. Before long, our car was jammed with women; not only was there no room to sit, but there was scarcely any room to stand. When the door was finally locked, we were practically one on top of another. We found ourselves in a dirty animal car with at least two hundred women. Above all, we had no water, no food, and we were given none during the journey. At first, we were stunned, and as a result there was hardly a sound in the freight car. At times we tried to sleep, but there was no room to rest our heads. Eventually, the five of us would take turns, and lean against each other. Anna was half-asleep most of the time. After a while we got used to the darkness and began to recognize the afflicted faces around us. Among the others, I spotted Mrs. B. and with great effort contrived to pull her near our little family group.

Soon after the shock at our situation was over, we started to complain; and our complaining was always interspersed with cries for water. Whenever the train came to a stop, we would beat on the door with all our might and cry out, trying to attract someone's attention, begging continually for a drop of water. But the door remained locked. The worst of it was the stench from urine and diarrhea, and soon it was almost impossible to breathe in the car.

When morning light crept through the small openings of the freight car walls, we could see that many women had fainted or died. There was no way to administer to the unconscious ones, and eventually, they, too, died. It looked as though the Germans had found a way of suffocating us all in these animal trains. Then, in surprising contrast to this misery, a solitary young voice burst out: "Why do you all give up? Why do you put your heads down and go to sleep, never to wake again? Have you forgotten that we have a God above who will help us? Did you children of Israel forget that He has saved our people so many times before and that He shall save us now? Do you want to die now, when the war is almost over? The Germans have suffered so many defeats that they cannot last much longer. I know it. I heard it from a German. Please believe me. Suffer, keep your heads up, if only a little longer!"

There was a dead silence in the wagon. Soon, another woman started to pray, then another, and we all repeated: "Adon Olam, Lord of the Universe . . . ."

Our prayers enveloped us sounding loud and clear. Our entire beings, our hearts were full of hope when we heard—to our disbelief and amazement—the roar of planes above. Could it be that they were American planes coming to save us? Perhaps they had learned about our transport and were following our creaking train to receive us all at the end and give us freedom, water, and food. It was remarkable; could it be true? We had heard rumors that the Americans were in the war against Germany, and we could think of only one reason why they would get involved in the war in Europe—to save the millions of people suffering in the German concentration camps.

My strength returned as I turned my thoughts now to America. America had always been a magic word to me for as long as I could remember. I had learned English in school, hoping that one day I would go to the United States and see that great country. The old folks were always talking about all the wonders of the world that America had. People who emigrated there after the First World War were describing scenes in their letters to their friends in Poland about the electric ovens, electric lights, the refrigeration, and the absolute richness of the country. The farmers were dreaming about the tractors America had, and the people in the cities dreamed about the cars every American possessed. And yet the greatest dream for all of us was that in America there was the embodiment of freedom for Jews, just as much as for everyone else. Whereas here in Poland, we had been oppressed for as long as one could remember.

When the sound of the planes came nearer, our hands went up in prayer. Once again, our confidence was entirely renewed. If they could only see us, we thought. Yet we knew that it could be otherwise, too; they might think the train carried German soldiers and supplies and bomb it. But even that would be an easier death than this suffocation. Death by a bullet would be a welcome relief, we thought. But the planes came and went, and we were still on the train gazing distractedly into the void—more depressed than ever after losing this little spark of hope.

The journey lasted two days, although we were unaware of it at the time. It seemed rather like two years, and our tongues were woolly from thirst. Mother was exhausted, yet relieved to be with us; my sisters and I had our youth to keep us alive. Mrs. B. tried to hide her pain and suffering from me by telling me stories about her beloved son. I numbly listened to her tales and knew how hopeless they were. Still, I was grieved by her plight and agreed to everything she said. One thing that worried me was that she was absolutely sure we were going to Auschwitz, and that she would see him there.

The thought that we were going to Auschwitz had been in our minds since the beginning of our journey, yet it seemed incredible that the Germans would go to the trouble of transporting us there to be killed in the gas chambers when they could so easily have finished us on this train.

Such thoughts, together with our fragmented feelings, drove us to a state bordering on madness. This I strove to overcome by losing myself in my memories. Thus, in my memories, I stumbled over the former images of my youth with a kind of recklessness: the rolling hills, the wintry mountain scenes, the beauty of my favorite haunts and retreats. Impulsively, desperately, I was trying to recapture that time now, somewhere, someplace, as it had been, as it would be despite all this, as well as the instinctive feeling I had always had that I would last forever, outlast the sea, the earth, and the war.

27 The sun was shining brightly, and our eyes couldn't get accustomed to the light as the door of the freight car was finally opened. A herd of SS men surrounded the train and pushed us out of the cars. Although, miraculously, many of us were still alive, numerous corpses were rolled out of the train and loaded onto waiting trucks.

We realized that we were, indeed, in Auschwitz. We had heard that here the Germans had to deliver a fixed number of Jews to the gas chambers every day. We also had heard that they collected Jewish teeth, hair, and other parts of Jewish bodies to be reduced into soap, brushes, and objects made of human skin. We had heard, too, that Jewish prisoners, chiefly girls, were used for so-called scientific experiments.

All these frightful thoughts flashed through our minds, filling us with tension, anger, and bewilderment. When we became accustomed to the light, we couldn't believe what we saw: a beautiful camp, new barracks, painted white, with lovely lawns and flowers. We heard soft music playing over the loudspeaker. The morning air was brisk, but the autumn sun endowed everything with warmth and hope that September morning.

"Mother, this can't be true!" I exclaimed.

"Don't you know how people like to exaggerate? This is a beautiful camp," Mother answered.

"We can have our own "five," the four of us and Mother. We shall go to work together, and everything will be fine," Anna added.

"Sure, everything will be fine," Pola said. "Look over there. Those people aren't joining our rows. Where are they taking them? Why aren't we going with them? We must be the ones going to the ovens! They are going to work. Look, look!" Pola almost shouted.

Indeed, another column was being formed away from ours. Mrs. B., my dear friend, rushed towards us from her column but was pushed by an SS man. She had survived this impossible journey, all the bitter disappointments, only because she hoped to see her son in Auschwitz. "If only I could see his face once more. If only I knew he was alive, I wouldn't mind dying. After all, I am old, very old, and he is so young. If only I could give my life so that he may live," she had said to me repeatedly during the journey.

As the SS guard confronted her now and pulled her into the other column, she called, "Take care . . of my son . ." I looked after her longingly. My voice failed me as a pain went through my heart, for I understood that she was parting from me forever. I had acquired a deeply genuine affection for her, and I enjoyed playing the part of her future daughter-in-law. She was a woman in her fifties, expecting so much from her doctor son, loving him, caring for him all these years. Now on her last journey, enduring so many torments, she had come to Auschwitz, hoping to find him. Her motherly intuition told her that she would never see him again when she said to me: "Take care of my son."

How absurd—take care of my son. Where could I find him? How would I recognize him? Not from the little picture she always showed me. The young high school boy in a uniform and a cap was so different from the young doctor I saw when the SS men pushed him onto the truck. Even though his face was blurred, the words I said to my father when I saw him being forced up onto the transport truck in the ghetto that day were still clear in my mind: "Look, Father, such a young handsome man is going to the oven." But perhaps I was wrong and she was right; perhaps he was alive. And if so, would I ever see him?

The four of us, with Mother, were headed into one column. The sun still shone, the music played on. The segregation continued, and at the moment, ours was the live column; the other one was destined to die. We had to believe it was so. We marched almost briskly to the tune of the "Edelweiss, my Edelweiss, will you live forever?" Would I?

We stopped near a huge building and were told to undress completely and leave all our belongings outside. There were at least five thousand of us after the segregation, and the field was crowded with naked women. We folded our clothes carefully, expecting to find them intact when we came back from what we concluded must be a huge bathhouse. Some women had been brought to Auschwitz directly from their homes. They had not been in concentration camps before, and therefore still had some valuables, such as jewelry, diamonds, or even American money. They had them sewn into their clothing, but having to undress completely presented a dilemma. Soon the women began inserting their valuables into their vaginas or rectums. One helped another to hide from the eyes of the SS men. These women had put their lives in jeopardy because it was strictly forbidden to have any valuables, and if found out, they would have been shot. But to some of them, these jewels meant buying their freedom, or even a slice of bread, and they considered it worth the risk.

"Let's get it over with," Pola urged.

"We'll take a shower, and then we shall go to work," Mania added.

Anna stood naked, looking smaller than she was, her huge eyes showing in her gaunt face and her skinny hands shaking. We remained together, and the four of us still with Mother, walked towards the door of the bathhouse. In front of the door stood two huge men in green uniforms, with green masks over their heads. Before we realized what was happening, the four of us were pushed into the building and Mother, thrown off guard, pulled in a different direction. As we stumbled into the building, we could hear: "You are too beautiful to live", or "You are too ugly to live"; "You have ugly feet"; "You are too old." He said whatever came to his mind, the green giant with the big green net around his head. He decided who was to live and who was to die. His was the final verdict.

Pulled and pushed from all sides by thousands of naked women, we were unable to grasp what was happening. I moved towards the window, holding on to Anna. Pola and Mania followed us with great effort. Through the window, we saw a column of hundreds of women standing in rows of five. "Order there must be!" the Germans shouted. I spotted Mother. I rushed towards the door; I wanted to get out, to be with her. I pushed, I shouted, I fought through the crowds to the door. But the green monster with the big mask shoved me back inside. My turn hadn't come yet. He didn't want me to have my wish come true. He would not let me go with my mother—my dear, wonderful, sweet, warm mother. She, too, struggled to make her way to me but was shoved back by her guards. All I could hear were her last words: "My angels, my dolls, may God help you——"

I returned to my sisters who were standing at the window and crying; we knew that we had seen our beloved mother for the last time. She stood there among the young and the old, the ugly and the beautiful, being counted and recounted; the Germans must have order, the count must be kept.

After her struggle, the suffering she had gone through, she was going to find her peace. I hoped and prayed that she would have a quick death. For days and months and years, even now the thought of her dying in the gas chambers lives in my memory, just like Mojshele before her; it penetrates my heart. The next day and every day after, I saw and still see their bodies crumbling down under the showers of the bathhouse in Auschwitz.

We wept for a moment, but we couldn't allow ourselves much thought at the time, for things were happening—terrible things—one after the other. There was no time to despair; in the confusion that followed one had to fight for life.

After the segregation, there must have been about four thousand of us left. We were all herded into a room no larger than twenty-by-twenty meters. Four thousand naked bodies, cringing, writhing, entangled together. No room to stand or to sit. One on top of the other—a foot in one's belly, a clenched hand wildly groping in another's hair. An ocean of contorted bodies in the most incredible juxtapositions: here a pair of eyes looking into emptiness, another one moaning from pain and hunger, a few struggling to get up from under the heap. Others, resigned, lay motionless with several bodies on top of them, the fear, the tragedy, the unbelievable strain showing in their faces. The half-dead corpses slowly surrendered what was left of life. No words came out of their mouths, no movement from their bodies. They had given up.

"How I wish we were with Mother," I heard Anna whisper, for she, too, had lost the shine in her eyes, which gazed vacantly about. There was hardly any life in her. She didn't care what happened; Mother wasn't with us any more. From now on there were only the four of us.

28 Deprived of all strength and the desire to live, confused and exhausted, we were pushed into another room. Before we had a chance to notice exactly what was happening, men with shavers began to shave our hair. One shaved our heads, another our underarms, and a young boy in a pair of shorts shaved the hair of our genitals. The men were experienced; it seemed to take no time at all. Oblivious to everything, we moved like robots from one shaver to another, yielding without a word. Nothing mattered any more. The long room was full of hair, some blond, some brown, some black. None was gray as there were no older women left among us. Then we were rushed into another room with showers.

After all we had gone through during the last few days, it seemed that it was the gas that would now finish us. We looked at each other, realizing what our destiny was to be at last. No one uttered a word; we were resigned and ready.

Suddenly the showers were opened, and freezing water rinsed our naked bodies. We were alive.

"Schnell! Raus! Raus!" the Germans shouted and chased us swiftly out of the shower room into the cold September dawn. Once we were outside, a garment was haphazardly and quickly thrown to us by men who stood on each side of us with a heap of clothes in front of them. The garments had to be put on in a flash. I caught a black evening gown. It had a low-cut back and an even lower front. As we had no underwear, my breasts were altogether exposed. Anna was thrown a pajama top; it scarcely covered her buttocks. I glanced for a second at Pola who looked a hundred years old in a long brown dress. Mania was lucky enough to catch a big skirt, which when put over her arms, covered her body completely.

As we proceeded through another line, a pair of wooden Dutch shoes were given to each of us. Most of them were big enough to put both feet in a single shoe. We put them on our wet feet which raised blisters and made each step extremely painful.

It was now morning. Our discolored bodies were covered in the most ridiculous garments, and with the queer wooden shoes on our feet, we were quite a sight. We walked in fives.

"How funny you look." Pola started laughing.

"And you, look at yourself!" Anna snapped.

"Stop it, girls. We all look funny, but we're alive, aren't we?" Mania said.

"Who cares? We might as well be dead," Pola answered.

"Stop it, will you?" I said sadly; for we had just turned off the muddy road and were marching in a different direction. All we could see, at a distance clearly visible against the morning sky was that in front of us, was fire. An ocean of fire. As far as the eye could see there was fire, and no other way to go. The hard morning light revealed a landscape dark with people and illuminated each vacant face.

"What a beautiful sight," Pola said acidly.

Behind us, a woman was holding her daughter's hand, and I heard her say: "After all we have been through . . . after this monstrous shaving . . . we have to go into the fire now?"

Her sixteen-year-old daughter replied calmly: "At least we shall be warm, Mother."

That was, in fact, how we all felt by now—a moving wall of broken-down forms driven by cold and despair.

Despite all this, to me the fire also meant something else—a tender reconciliation with my mother. In each little flame, I saw her kisses, her love, gliding toward me then heavenward. I heard her last words: "My angels, my dolls, may God help you." We knew, now, that she must have been taken into the gas chamber during the night, and it was her body along with thousands of others, young and old, beautiful and ugly, that was burning in this inferno.

And somewhere, too, through the searing flames, I could see the last worry on my dearest friend's face, when she said to me: "Take care of my son." She, also, must have found her tragic end last night. I thought of how the two women had died together.

We were now just a few steps away from the barbed wire separating us from the fire. At any given moment, the gate would open and we would be led into the fire where violent red flames were sending blue flecks into the dark, smoke-filled sky. It appeared that the Germans were playing tricks on us. During the last few days we had died an innumerable number of deaths: at first, the suffocation on the train, then the segregations, afterward, the showers, and now a fire. Most of us had experienced something akin to dying each time, and it was as if part of us had died each time. Yet, this wasn't going to be the last time either. As soon as we were almost so close that there seemed to be no turning from it, we were led onto a different road and away from the fire. Nevertheless, the Germans had accomplished their goal, for in that fire, a great part of our souls had been obliterated—the part of us that knew how to love, respect, and hope. Here was where our parents, our brothers and sisters, and most of our friends had died. We knew now what the gas chambers of Auschwitz had meant. As we moved away from the fire, the smell of burning corpses stayed with us all through our march—as it would stay all through our stay in Auschwitz. Whether the smell was of freshly burned bodies or carried over from previous burnings, it was always there, and we could never help but be aware of it.

29 The fire did not consume us physically, yet something had happened to me. I felt as if the whole inside of my body was taken out and the remainder—that is, the outer body, the legs and the eyes—were marching on.

I could not feel anything. I tried to tell myself that my mother had just been taken from me, yet I didn't feel the loss. I tried to tell myself that Tola, Henia, and Renia, my very best friends, had been taken away, segregated, and were probably burning in that fire, yet I still had no feeling of loss. All I could feel was the discomfort of the wooden Dutch shoes on my feet and the cold air on my exposed breasts.

I must also add that as I looked around at my sisters and the others and saw the funny clothes they were wearing, I couldn't help but laugh. Somebody pointed out: "Hanka, that evening dress fits you beautifully." I looked at her and began to laugh hysterically. Hanka was short and the dress was long; she had to hold it up to avoid tripping over it. The funniest part was that with our hair shaven completely, we looked rather like little hairless monkeys.

I shall never forget the way my sister Anna looked. She had been handsome. Her features were strong but not coarse, her nose straight, her mouth well shaped and not too small. Her great beauty lay in her eyes. They were exceedingly clear, the black and white pure and separate. When I looked at her now, all I could see were the white and black of her eyes. They looked like two large balls attached to a bony face with long legs. With her dark hair shaven, her scalp was very white. The striped pajama top she had been given scarcely covered her buttocks, and her long legs wobbled in wooden shoes of two different sizes. I cursed the Dutch for making them. They added considerably to our misery. When we put them on at night, our feet were wet and cold. By the time we had taken a few steps, the skin of

123

our feet was rubbed off, and we could hardly walk. Yet we marched, we marched to the beat of the SS men's boots. We arrived in Birkenau, Lager B2B.

I didn't know how long we marched or where or how far. I had no feelings, no desire to live, or to die. I was just numb.

When I found myself lying down, I went to sleep. I think I could have slept forever if it hadn't been for the whistles blowing, noises, and shouts all around me. When I came to, I was told that it was four o'clock in the morning and we had to go outside.

My sister Pola took my hand and pulled me along with her. In no time, we were standing in fives. A young girl who couldn't have been more than fifteen, chubby with red cheeks and her hair combed neatly, blew the whistle. "Undress!" she shouted.

She was what we called a "Capo." The Germans didn't want to waste their manpower in small positions, so they trained the prisoners to do the dirty work for them. Most of the inmates of Auschwitz were dehumanized to such an extent that it didn't matter what kind of work they did, as long as they could get a little more food and a bed they didn't have to share with twelve other people. At a time when nothing else mattered and the chance for survival was becoming less and less, the job of being a Capo was the last straw. Not everybody could stomach behaving like a monster, punishing their own people and, as at Auschwitz, quite often sending them to the gas chambers. But there were those who did take the job—some by choice, and many others selected by the Germans.

In seconds we had freed ourselves of our clothing—there were no undergarments, of course—and stood naked. We had stood like that the first day and would for many days to come. When nobody was watching us, we would sit down for a moment. But no sooner had we begun to rest when the voice of the Devil behind that angelic face screamed; "Get up! stand up!"

The Capo had a whip in her hand and always let us know she meant business. The whip would flick our naked bodies and burn like hell. We couldn't figure her out. She spoke Czech, so she must have been from Czechoslovakia. She was very young, and at first we couldn't understand what made her so vicious toward us. Every now and then I would try to talk to her, and she would look at me, seemingly friendly, but just when I thought she was ready to say something to me, she would shout: "Go away, go away, before I punch you!"

Later we learned that she had been one of the early comers to Auschwitz and had been chosen to dig a grave for her parents and her sisters. For a while, she had worked in the crematorium. She had been educated to be tough. The poor soul didn't even know why she did what she did.

At noon, we were given a bowl of soup. At first, we were reluctant to drink it because we were told that it had some medication in it to stop us from menstruating. Some said that we would lose our womanhood completely. We didn't understand what that meant, but we knew it was bad. The first day I wouldn't touch the soup, but the next day my stomach was cramping so terribly that I swallowed the soup with delight. We didn't menstruate, and what a blessing it was under those circumstances.

When evening came, we were allowed to go into the barracks. The barracks were located in Birkenau, which was a suburb of Auschwitz and its actual transit camp. The barracks were very long and filled with beds, one three-decker close to another. Each bed was the size of a regular double bed, and on each slept twelve people. When night came, we tried to find a comfortable position, which was quite a chore. If we lay next to one another, we had no room to breathe. If we lay alternating head down and feet up, we were kicked continuously. If we had to turn at night, we had to do it simultaneously.

Eventually we developed a routine. Everybody was dead tired at night, and we just slept, if they let us. Unfortunately, they decided that the best time for us to stand outside was at four o'clock in the morning, and when the whistle blew, we had to line up in fives outside.

This gave some kind of added pleasure to our Capo, and she practiced it every night. When a prisoner was too slow in getting into her row, she was forced to stand all day or had her bowl of soup taken away from her.

I began to have nightmares and was obsessed with the thought that I might not get my bowl of soup, that my stomach would begin to cramp again; I knew I couldn't stand it anymore. I was so possessed by hunger and my own feelings that I didn't even think about my sisters. At times I realized that I didn't care whether anyone was dead or alive, just as long as I could get the bowl of soup to keep me going.

"Ruth, Ruth, I know you aren't asleep. Why can't you talk to me?" Anna whispered, but I wouldn't answer her. I felt numb.

Slowly, however, the daily routine got under my skin, and I began to feel things. When Mania was punished, I realized that I cared. I didn't speak to her, but I tried to find a way of letting her know that I cared. She wasn't to have anything to eat for twenty-four hours. She had been separated from us all day, but when evening came, she was already on the bed waiting for us. "I have to tell you something," she said in a low voice. "The Devil (as we all called the Capo by now) wants me to sew something for her. When she punished me, I managed to talk to her. I told her I could sew, and she will have something for me tomorrow."

"You are kidding," Pola murmured. She never believed anything good could happen to us.

Sure enough, the next morning my sister was standing naked outside and sewing a dress for the Devil. Every time an inspection was made, we had to hide it, but as it didn't belong to us, we weren't too concerned. We knew the Devil would cover for it.

Since our routine was to stand outside all day and wait for segregations, we stood that day and helped Mania sew. In the evening, the dress was ready and, after delivery, Mania came back with a huge slice of bread. What a feast! We each had a bite. We were beginning to live.

The next day the Devil brought another piece of material, with white and blue checks for a blouse. Of course, she had to supply us with scissors, needles, and thread, which she did. We sewed again, and again we had a slice of bread. This time it was an even greater joy. Besides getting a piece of bread, Mania was able to cut a piece of material and fill in the cut-out of my dress where my breasts were showing. In spite of everything, I felt much better at not being so exposed.

Next to our camp, separated by heavy barbed wire, was a camp of men. They must have been hungry, hungry for food and women. They stood there and stared at us all day. There was nothing else they could do. We were there, and they were right next to us. They had to look. Strangely enough, we didn't mind. We were all women from fourteen to about forty, yet we didn't mind having the men look at our naked bodies day in and day out because we didn't feel like women. What could they possibly see in a skeleton-like body without hair? Also, the fact that we didn't know any of them made a difference.

One day I learned that Mark, my dear friend who had been taken out of the ghetto with his father, was in Auschwitz. I wondered if he had heard of his mother's suicide, but I wasn't going to mention it. He was an electrician and was coming to our camp. "How am I going to face him?" I asked my sisters. "I can't let him see me like this!"

"What is all this talk? For months you have been standing out here, showing off to all the men, and now that Mark is coming you make such a fuss," Pola snapped.

"Pola, please stop it. These men don't mean anything to me. Mark is different."

"Don't worry, darling, we'll make you look beautiful," Mania added. Her sewing came in handy again. She was making a skirt for another Capo, and she cut a piece of material to make a scarf for me. With my dress patched and the blue scarf covering my bald head, I looked like a girl again.

Suddenly I wanted to look attractive and act human, mainly, I think, because Mark had known me when I was young and pretty, and I wanted to look the same to him. He loved me, he had said so many times. The night we went to the concert in the ghetto, he had held my hand and kissed me. I could still feel it. What does he look like after two years in Auschwitz? Does he still have any feelings, especially for a girl, for me? So many thoughts went through my mind.

Morning came, and again we all had to stand outside naked and shivering. It was the end of October, and the air was very cold and windy.

Finally, the day of Mark's visit arrived. He was coming to repair the electric wiring in one of the barracks, and I was to meet him there. Mania tied the little blue square over my bald head, and one could hardly see that I had no hair. "You look beautiful," my sister Anna said. "He loves you anyhow," Pola added.

My heart beat fast as I walked into the barrack. I saw him; it was easy to spot a man among hundreds of women. He came towards me. He recognized me. My knees trembled; for a moment, I was ready to turn back and run.

"Hello, Ruth," he said slowly, looking at me intensely. He can see through me, I thought. It seemed as if he would eat me up with his eyes. He stared at me without saying a word. I moved towards him and kissed him on the cheek. He touched my face like a blind person. He couldn't believe it was really I.

"Your father, your sister," I managed to say. He glared up into the skies. I understood.

"I brought you a toothbrush," he whispered and handed it to me.

"Mark, how much longer can this last? What do you think?" I asked.

"Not much longer. The Russians are coming, for sure," he answered quickly and took me in his arms, hugging me and kissing my forehead. "Ruth, listen, it won't be long. You must be strong. Try not to register for any outside commandos. The Russians are not far; we can even hear them. A Capo told me it won't be long. Please, Ruth, you must live," he said, holding me so tightly I ached. But I didn't mind that it hurt. He cared for me. And he had even offered me hope. I hadn't thought of that word for ages. As a matter of fact, I didn't even think about the future anymore. It was meaningless when all I cared about was surviving the tortures of each day.

I soon left Mark, afraid that someone might discover me. I joined my row of fives, took the scarf off my head, and once again stood naked. But deep inside, something that I had thought was dead was being born again—the will to live.

30 A freezing wind was blowing, and our naked bodies felt stiff as we stood in fives between the two blocks. We sensed that something was going to happen this day. The air was so clear and so quiet.

When the sun came out, we were told to put on our clothes and march. Our own five, which consisted permanently of Pola, Anna, Mania, a girl named Wanda, and me, held hands. The others looked at me, wanting to know where we were going, but I just held my head high and let them guess. The truth was, I didn't know where we were going, but what the others didn't know was that I now believed nothing bad could happen to us anymore. No gas chambers for us; we had to outlive this war.

After a short march, with hardly a word, we stopped in an open place, the Appellplatz. In the middle of it, we noticed tables and girls sitting at them. For a split second, the word segregation crossed my mind, but I quickly dismissed it.

I soon realized that we were going to be numbered, a procedure we had already heard about from other inmates of Auschwitz. My mind started to work very fast. I knew that when they tattooed us, they would also register us according to name and age. There was a quick family conference. What we decided must be kept secret; even our best friends shouldn't know about it. We didn't trust anybody in Auschwitz; hunger had a way of bringing about irrational behavior in people.

We couldn't register as sisters, that was for certain. They didn't cater to family affairs in Auschwitz. Another problem: Anna and Pola were too young for Auschwitz, that is, too young to live, according to the SS commander. One decision: Anna, slender as she was, would pass for sixteen and register under the name, Anna Weitz; Pola would be seventeen, and register under the name of Krantz; Mania would register as Rubin, age nineteen, and I would retain my own name and age.

I could see my sisters' lips moving as they tried to

remember who was who. Then their turns came and they were registered. When it was my turn, I felt the burn of the pen as one point after another the number A-19348 was branded into my flesh. I was to be a number from now on, Number A-19348 forever after.

Curiously, as a number it was easier to cope. Stripped of clothing, feelings, moral obligations, and human qualities, one was better off being a number.

I returned to the block. As Number A-19348, I automatically reached for my soup, a bowl of cold water of scarcely any consistency at all. I looked at the Capo who spooned it out for me, and strangely enough, I wasn't even mad at her. I drank it, and empty and as hungry as ever, made my way to my bed. Even that looked different. When we first came, it had had some straw on it, but that was gone by now. There was only an empty wooden board about six feet long and six feet wide, where twelve numbers went to sleep every night. Sleep was a welcome time, and nobody felt discomfort anymore. Our bony bodies needed less room, and when someone died during the night or in the course of the day, we felt lucky because there was a little more room. And people were dying fast.

Wanda, the young girl who completed our five, was a timid young lady. She was from an upper-class family. They had lived in the best part of town and had even had a car, which before the war was quite something in Poland. Her father had been a bank director, and Wanda was an only child. She could make up beautiful poems, and sometimes one had the feeling that a part of her was somewhere else. She spoke beautifully. She, however, had one bad habit: she couldn't stand hunger. This poor girl suffered dreadfully. Her cramps were so violent that she would curl in half. Her face grew smaller and smaller. She slept next to us, and when I looked at her, I saw a distant look in her eyes.

Wanda had always stayed near us as if drawing from the warmth of our love for each other. She, too, wanted someone to worry about her, and this we did. She was the one who got a piece of bread here and there, when Mania was sewing, but for all we did, it wasn't enough.

One night, Pola woke me gently. "Ruth, Ruth, look," she said sadly, with a lamenting voice as she pointed to Wanda. I touched the girl; she was quite cold. "Poor Wanda, she will never make it now," I said. Accustomed as we were to this sort of thing, Pola and I still couldn't sleep that night.

"You know, Ruth, she was such a gentle flower, too gentle for this kind of life," Pola whispered, tears rolling down her cheeks. "Ruth, why don't we talk—I mean talk about Mother and Father? What is it? I can't understand it. Sometimes it chokes me so that I think I won't be able to take another breath; then I hear the whistle blow and the order, 'dress,' 'undress,' 'march,' and I just do it. Ruth, what is happening to all of us?"

Without waiting for my answer, Pola continued: "Do you remember the times at home when we sat at dinner and ate quickly, without a word, anxious to finish because there was something more exciting, more beautiful waiting for us? Like Lolek rushing off to his house and coming right back after dinner to spend the evening with you. Ruth, do you remember?"

"Yes, I remember. Poor Lolek. Who knows what has happened to him? He was my first love when I was still in school. That was a million years ago."

"Did you know," Pola went on "that one day Anna and I watched you kiss Lolek. I remember, you went to play tennis with him early in the morning. We got dressed soon after you left and followed you to the park. You played for quite a while, and Anna was getting angry. She wanted to go home; she thought it was stupid to watch you and Lolek. Of course, she was only nine. But I wanted to wait. I didn't really know why or what it was I wanted to see, but I had watched you with Lolek and you seemed so happy. Then it happened. You had finished playing. Anna was sitting in the bushes, but I still followed you. Lolek put his arms around you and kissed you. I could almost hear your bones crack. Anna got up, her mouth wide open; she pulled my hand and started to run. I ran, too. I ran because I felt badly, taking your secret away from you.

"Ruth, are you listening? Did you really enjoy those kisses? If they were as pleasant as they looked, I wish I could experience some."

I put my hand on hers and stroked it. "You will, my child, you will." I kissed her and we went to sleep. Pola moved closer to me, away from the cold body of Wanda.

One morning we were standing outside, naked, ready for

the selection. Even though on some days they just came, looked us over, and went on to another block, we knew that our time would come, too.

This was the day. Armed from head to toe, they came, three of them. Their stern faces and their looks froze the blood in our veins. They were doing the choosing. "You, and you, and you, and you."

The four of us found ourselves among the "you's." About sixty women were chosen; for what, nobody knew. It could have been the gas chamber. A lot of women were crying that night. Were we going to the gas chambers, or were they?

In any case, we were going to be separated again. One thing that bothered me though, was that if they wanted us for the gas chamber, why not send us at once? I had to put these thoughts out of my mind, however, because I knew by now that the Germans had their own way of doing things, and nothing was simple, not even death in a gas chamber.

How strange everything seemed the next morning. It was raining for the first time since our arrival at Auschwitz. Usually a rainy season in Poland, September had been dry as if for our sakes. We couldn't take rain under the circumstances in which we lived, yet we wanted rain for the sake of the war. We knew the Germans couldn't advance in rain. We were really all mixed up about the rain. When the rumors had reached us that the Americans were in the war, we wanted them to come in herds and bomb the whole of Germany, even if we had to go with it. How many times, I remembered later on, we wished the next bomb would be for us.

We were formed in fives and marched off. Despite the cold and rain, I was glad that we were all together again—Mania, Anna, Pola, and I. We didn't speak; we had nothing to say. I thought about the things Pola had said to me the night Wanda died.

On that march, however, we were all dead. A mass of dead bodies marching somewhere to the tune of the SS men's boots. Where? Nobody even gave it a thought.

We soon left the gates of B2B and were outside; not outside of Auschwitz, but it was a different world we walked into. The barracks were clean and painted, with little gardens all around them. The grass was green and the hedges were made of flowers. It was almost too beautiful for words. After standing between the two barracks at Birkenau for a month on hard, cold ground, with no sign of grass, or a leaf, this looked like paradise.

"Who were the lucky ones?" we wondered.

After marching for what seemed an eternity, and was probably only a couple of kilometers, we were brought to a stop in front of a bathhouse. It was quite different from the bathhouse we had experienced on our arrival in Auschwitz. They must have built this one recently. It must be a new one they built, we thought.

"Why don't they take us in and get it over with," Anna lamented, pulling my hand.

"Don't be in such a hurry. Where you're going, you'll always have time," the girl next to her said.

Twenty girls went in while the rest of us waited. When the order came to go in, the four of us tried to squeeze in together. We did not want to be separated even in death; that was one thing we knew. We took off our clothes and were headed into the shower room.

I could hardly believe my eyes when I saw water dripping from the faucet. As I looked around, I saw the expressions on the faces of the girls change, muscles relaxed.

When I felt the warm water slide over my body, I wanted to stand there forever. The warmth felt so good on the cold body. The water felt so soothing and the cake of soap we were all sharing gave softness and cleanness to our bodies. We washed our scalps, which were beginning to roughen where new hair was beginning to grow.

Gently, I went over my skinny body. The warmth and the softness I was experiencing was so delightful that I wouldn't have minded going to the gas chamber.

There was something we couldn't understand. For the first time since we had been in camp, we were left alone, and for a long while, too.

A woman came and ordered us into another room. There, we were given different clothes. It was a relief to get rid of my evening gown. The dresses we received were neater and cleaner and a little bit warmer.

When we returned to Birkenau that evening, we had a lot to talk about. The other women looked at us in awe. We still didn't know why we had been granted this great privilege.

The next morning we went to work. New barracks were being built, and we were to carry the stones for the buildings. We didn't mind the work because it gave us a chance to get away from our own barracks and the tension: will they pick me today? Besides, we had contact with others who worked there. And there were men. We had very little chance to talk, but when the guards weren't looking we managed to learn that the Americans and the Russians were coming closer; that the war should be over very soon and Germany would definitely be defeated.

A young boy was following me. "What is your name?" he asked.

"I am Ruth Bachner, from Krakow."

"I am Julek Sapinski. Listen, Ruth, don't let this break you, it won't last long," he said.

I shook my head, for I understood how he felt. He was new at the game. Auschwitz was the first camp he had been sent to. They gave him work, he even wore his own clothes. How little he knew.

The next day, he approached me again. "Did you hear? The Russians are coming. It is just a question of surviving the next few days." Before he finished, a guard with a whip came over and swung it at his body. Julek, I wanted to scream, but I only bit my tongue, for another lash of the whip struck his body. Julek went on working, giving me wild glances.

There was something in his eyes I had not seen for a long time: hatred, a fighting spirit, something that had been killed in us. This boy wasn't thinking about how to survive to the next day; his mind was working on how to kill a few Germans before he would have to surrender. Was he real? I wondered.

My doubts were soon answered. After we arrived at work the next morning, we were told to remain in fives and then ordered to march towards the wires. We marched head down, knowing that something would happen soon. This was too good—working, getting a bowl of soup every day, and sleeping peacefully, without roll calls, without segregation. This must be the end of it.

I heard the familiar whistle.

"Achtung! Stand still, heads up!"

My head up and my eyes opened, I knew now what awaited us. Crumpled between the wires was a human body;

how tiny it seemed! A small bundle of clothes, still holding onto the wire. It was the last remains of Julek Sapinski, a young boy, enemy of the German Reich.

"Look, look well! He wanted freedom. You have all the freedom you're going to get here, you Jewish swine, don't you know that yet?" the SS man screamed. "You should all hang, you Jewish swine. You don't know how good the Führer is to you."

"Anyone disregarding orders will meet the same destiny. Remember, don't you try anything funny. Those wires are electric, or didn't you know it?" he yelled.

"Get to work, quick, we are wasting time!" he added. I worked the next few days automatically.

31 It was 11 November. What a memorable day! In Poland, it was the day of Independence. Could it be that only five years ago—and not a century—I marched in fives in a school procession to celebrate this significant event? We wore our school uniforms of navy blue with white starched collars. I was always placed in the first line; they said I was a good representative for the school because I was tall, good looking, and wore clothes well.

Some of my classmates had teased me, saying that it was my blond hair that attracted attention to our school as we marched. Whatever it was that gave me the honor, I liked it.

We would march to the Tomb of the Unknown Soldier, and I would place the wreath on it. I remember that this was the only time I could go near a grave and not to be afraid. There was something wonderful about an unknown soldier, some-thing that gave me a feeling of pride, of respect. I didn't see him buried under the ground, six feet deep; I saw him standing erect, six feet tall.

I felt differently about other dead people, however. Ever since I was a little girl, I had been afraid to go near a cemetery. I even feared the word 'die,' or 'dead.' The sound of those words always brought back the face of my beloved grandmother. I was only ten years old when she died, but I loved her dearly. When I saw her face in the casket, it frightened me terribly. I ran away screaming, and I had been afraid ever since. I could never forgive my father for letting me see her dead.

I was no longer that girl who shrank from the sight of dead people. I now had seen hundreds of dead people and had no fears nor even feeling. Did my sisters feel the same way? These were my thoughts as we stood on this cold November morning between our barracks, again naked, exposed to the freezing wind and to a new crop of men who had arrived behind the barbed wire. The wires which separated our barracks from the men's were ordinary wires and not electric. The men stood staring, their eyes bulging, tongues hanging. Who were they? Where had they come from?

"Ruth, look. Do you see what I see?" whispered Mania, pointing in the direction of one of the men.

"Who is he? Do we know him?" I asked.

Pola was listening and looking, too. "Ruth, please don't look," she begged. "Don't let him see us."

"He won't recognize us anyhow," Mania quickly added.

"That is Jack Levy, a Capo from Plaszow," Mania explained.

"Ruth, let's ask him about Father. Maybe he knows something," Pola said in a trembling voice.

"Achtung! Achtung!" The whistle blew. We stood at attention; the men quickly retreated from the wires and watched us from afar.

What was going to happen now, I wondered. I knew something was coming up, for they weren't sending us to work. Was it the selection again? Were we the next candidates for the ovens? Come on and get it over with—the sooner the better!

What was it Pola had said, that Jack might know something about Father? Where was Father? Why are we afraid to talk about it, or even think about our parents? Are we afraid of more pain? The gas will cure all that.

"Ruth, what will happen to me?" I heard the frightened voice of Anna in back of me. "Anna, Annele, don't cry, darling. Whatever happens to us will happen to you. We've managed to be together so far, haven't we? Leave it to me," I said.

"I know what you mean. If they take me to the oven, you will go with me. You can't do that; you mustn't. Oh, Ruth," she wailed.

Pola and Mania came closer. We all formed one human bundle. We didn't even need to say it. We all knew why Anna was so upset. Two days before, she had broken out in a rash. It was vividly red now, and I knew there was no way to hide it. It looked like scarlet fever but she didn't feel sick.

If only they wouldn't come today; if only Anna could have one more day! Perhaps the spots would disappear. If only she could go to the infirmary for help. But what if they made her stay there? Then she would be dead for sure. God help me to find a way out of this!

What was happening to me? This was the first time I had

called for God's help in a long time. Had I forsaken Him, or had He forsaken us? Before we came to Auschwitz, I hardly ever fell asleep without saying a prayer, and now? Now, I couldn't even pray. I was afraid of finding out there is no God. In desperation, I must find help—I must. Even if He is very, very far away, He might hear me. He is my only hope right now. Even if He would arrange it so that we all had the rash, that wherever we were destined to go, we all would go together. But not just Anna, not my little Anna.

God, she has hardly lived. She has had so little time. How can she die without ever again seeing the glory of stars at night, the innocence of morning, the sunrise, the smell of the flowers, the glitter of sunlight on roughened waters of the Sola river? Without hearing the laughter of her beloved, or feeling the love he will have for her? Oh, Anna, my dear Anna, how I wish I could let you feel it all. Deep, deep inside, I can still feel the emotion of love. It was there after all; it wasn't taken away from me; for not even Hitler's army, or his gas chambers, could take away what was inside me.

We stood in silence. The Blockelteste with her whip came shouting and yelling. "Anziehen! Schnell! Schnell!" As soon as we had put on our garments, we followed her in fives. As we marched towards the Appellplatz we could see an ocean of humanity there already. What a sight! The scalps shaven, the dresses hanging as if on iron hangers. The only visible feature in anybody's face was the nose. The eyes were still shining in a few, but most were clouded with sorrow and grief.

In the middle of the Appellplatz, a few tables could be seen and a lot of green uniforms—some kind of high brass. The Capos, all women, screamed and yelled and exercised their long whips on anybody and everybody. We held hands tightly.

Every now and then I glanced at Anna. Her eyes were red from crying. How fortunate that her burning body is covered with that yellow rag she is wearing, I thought.

"Ruth, there must be at least five thousand women here today. What are they going to do to us?" Mania whispered.

There was hardly any time for thinking. Things were happening very fast. Women were walking in all directions.

Suddenly in front of our lines: "Twenty beautiful, intelligent women for work," the SS man shouted. He walked past our line:

"Du Schöne, intelligente?" And as he said it, he pulled first Mania, then Pola and me. On he went, until he had chosen twenty women. The Capo pulled us in front of the SS men's table and told us to take off our dresses so we could be inspected. I pulled off my dress and turned in panic; Anna wasn't with us. I looked at my sisters and knew what I had to do. I ran out of the line, through the crowds, through the yelling Capo's whip, to where Anna was still standing. Without thinking, I tore off her dress and pulled her with me where the row of twenty women were standing. I held her hand tightly, and even though the whip hit right between us, it didn't separate us. I tried to get inside the row, for I knew that we had to be somewhere in the middle of the line, or one of us would be the twenty-first. The shouts and kicking of the other girls didn't stop me, didn't even bother me. We had to be together.

One look told me that all they were looking for was healthy bodies. In my panic, lo and behold, I had completely forgotten about Anna's rash. What had I done? Now they would take her, for sure. Oh Lord, what are we to do? In a panic, I looked at Anna, and I couldn't believe my eyes.

"Anna, look!" I whispered, indicating her body with my eyes. At that moment, she stood erect, for the SS man already had his eyes on her. After he had passed her, he went on to me, then the next, and the next. Twenty were counted; the last one returned to the crowd. When he had finished and was talking to the other man, I couldn't help but kiss Anna tenderly. "Oh, Anna, do you see your body? The rash has disappeared. Thank you, Lord," I added in a whisper.

As we walked back to the barracks, the only thing we could talk about was the disappearance of the rash. Anna talked excitedly. "Can you imagine, when you were picked out of the lines, I only had one thought, to be together with you, no matter whether we were picked for the gas chamber or what. I forgot completely about my rash! Look, look, Mania, Pola, I have no rash. My body is completely clean. I can't believe it!" She went on talking.

"I think it was a miracle," Mania said enthusiastically. "And I'll tell you something else. Since one miracle has happened, it can mean only one thing."

"What do you mean?" Pola asked. "She means," I

answered, "that another miracle will soon happen. We shall get out of Auschwitz."

"You must be kidding. Or maybe you know something we don't know?" Pola inquired.

"I still can't forget what happened today. Let's not worry about tomorrow. The main thing is, we are together, thanks to Ruth," Anna concluded.

As we arrived at the barrack, women were coming in. Some had been chosen, others not. Nobody could explain what it meant or whether it was better to be chosen or not chosen.

I remembered the sparkle in Julek's eyes when he told me it wouldn't be much longer. Perhaps it would be better to remain in Auschwitz. The Russians would come here soon. On the other hand, maybe it was better to get out. I had a feeling that before the Russians or anybody else came, the Germans would leave no trace of Auschwitz or of us.

We were just as much afraid of victory as of defeat. Every time German troops suffered at the front, we were made to suffer also in one way or another. The gas chambers functioned day and night. One might naturally wonder where this enormity of evil had come form, but we didn't give it a thought. We were too busy trying to survive. Things were happening too fast in Auschwitz, and there was no time for thinking.

One thing was certain: when we first came to the camp, we knew a lot of people in our barracks. By now, we had very few friends. Most of them had been removed either dead or alive, and only a handful remained.

Tomorrow might bring another selection.

32 On the morning of 16 November, we were lined up in front of our barracks but this time with our clothes on. We stood there for hours, and every now and then our Capo would come out and tell us to stand erect. Between her visits, however, we had a chance to communicate with the men across the wire. Pola sneaked out of our row and was back soon.

"I talked to Jack; he said Plaszow was liquidated," she said in one breath.

"What do you mean liquidated?" Mania almost yelled.

"Just what I said—liquidated. Go ask him." Before I could say something, Mania was on her way, and we all followed. Jack was staring at us as if we were creatures from another planet.

"Ruth, for goodness sake, is that you? And you, Mania, and Anna, Pola? Oh, God." He put his hand across his eyes.

"It's us all right. Tell us what you know about Father," I asked him.

"I don't know, but he must have been sent away. You see, they sent away a lot of transports in different directions, and then some remained, and many others were shot to death. I know, because I was one of the last to leave. I can tell you it was no picnic. But how is it you are here, I mean, alive?" Jack looked at us. "We were told the whole transport was——" We didn't wait to hear the end of Jack's tale; we ran back into the lines because the Devil had blown her whistle again.

This time, the twenty of us who had been chosen the day before were ordered to march. I looked around at the girls I had lived with for the last few weeks and wondered if we or they were to enter the gas chambers of Auschwitz first? I saw tears on Lola's and Fela's cheeks. The girls were crying for us. Every time someone left the barracks, it was most likely for the gas chambers.

Pola, Anna, Mania, and I held hands, and Tola was the fifth

of our five. The march was slow, and only two guards were with us. Nobody spoke a word. There was silence around us, and the smell of burning bodies penetrated our senses.

We passed different areas of barracks, all separated from each other by wires. We even passed the beautiful, clean barracks with little gardens we had so admired on our first arrival in Auschwitz. We knew now that this was one area we didn't want to be in. These barracks were for the young and beautiful, who had been chosen for medical experiments. The best specimens of the human race. How ironic that they could stay in beautiful barracks with grass all around but had to suffer such a destiny. We heard that some of the girls who had been taken from our barracks were there. They had been sterilized. What a future for a young woman! Even if she survived the war, she would not be able to bear children. Yet didn't we all share the same fate? After all, we no longer menstruated; we had been given medicine for that. How did we know it wouldn't affect us forever?

After marching for hours, it seemed, we were brought again into a bathhouse. As we walked past the gates, we noticed a group of women standing there. The guards left us alone, and we surrounded the girls immediately.

"Gienia," Anna screamed, and kissed the tall, long-legged girl.

"Gienia," Pola echoed, and we all gathered around her.

"We came from Nachrichten Gerette Lager, and we are going to work for the same company in Germany," she explained.

"You mean, we are going with you? How many are you?"

"Eighty."

Mania shouted: "That must be it, don't you see? They need a hundred schöne intelligente frauen. That is it. Imagine, I can't believe it."

"Have you lost your head completely? Can't you see how they are dressed, and look at Gienia's beautiful hair?" Anna pointed.

I looked at the long-legged Gienia, with beautiful black curly hair falling down her back, a lovely dress on and a traveling bag in her hand. She used to share a bunk in Plaszow with us. Now she really looked as though she were going places. And we, our heads shaven, dirty, with worn-out dresses, and no underwear, —where else could we go if not to the gas chambers?

The eighty girls all looked neat and clean. They were working for a good outfit, they said. The captain was good to them and he was taking them to Germany to work for him. If we could get in on that deal, we would be lucky, they said.

"We sure will be lucky," Pola went on, smoothing her scalp, a little color showing on it already. Perhaps it was the wind and the sun, and maybe a few roots were coming up.

The guards came out, and the eighty girls were told to enter the bath chambers. The twenty of us just stood there speechless. We were envious, really envious. As long as we were together with thousands of women who looked the same as we did, we were happy. Perhaps not happy, but surely we didn't even pay attention to our looks or the lack of them. Suddenly here we were exposed to a group of women who had hair, who looked like human beings, and we felt like little, skinned animals. If only we could have crawled under the ground, we would have done just that. As I looked at our little group, I noticed that almost instantly every one of the women was touching her head to see if the hair was growing yet; unfortunately, it grew very, very slowly.

From another entrance we were invited into the bath chambers. There was, indeed, a real bath. I think we must have felt that our destiny was other than the gas chambers, or we wouldn't have been so terribly worried about our looks. The showers were delightful. Warm water, soap. After we had finished, we received a bundle of clothes. What a change! Underwear! Nothing ever felt as good as the pair of underpants I put on after that warm bath. My insides were cold, cold all the way through, and those panties, as I dared to call them, for they were big and rough textured, really felt good. Each of us got a blue-and-white-striped dress. The dress had long sleeves and the fabric was heavy. We looked at one another with delight. Anna and Mania switched dresses for size, but otherwise the dresses fit and we were warm.

The sun was shining as we walked out of the bath. Standing in front of us were eighty women with heads shining light and bright in the sun. I almost screamed. I couldn't believe my eyes. As we came closer, we began to laugh. We were hysterical. We simply roared. The laughing caught on, and pretty soon, we were all laughing hysterically. We looked at the bald heads and howled.

"Gienia," Anna pointed at her head. The black, long, curly hair was gone and she was standing erect with her white scalp shining in the sun.

"Don't worry," Anna added, "look at mine, it is growing a little already."

"You see, mine isn't as white as yours any more," Mania added.

We all mixed together. We felt like a group. A sudden feeling of togetherness existed between us. We were all alike. We belonged together. We knew now we were going to the same working place in Germany and we felt good inside. When we were told to form fives again, Gienia was the fifth for ours.

As we left the gates, we could see a railway station with a lot of trains, not passenger trains, of course, but animal cars, and we knew that they would be our destination now. How different it felt when we were boarding the train. How different from the time only two months ago when we were thrown out of those trains. Two months, and it seemed like eternity. Even Anna didn't look like the baby of the family anymore. She was skinny all right, but she had grown in spite of everything, and she had that mature look in her eyes.

Pola, on the other hand, seemed to be swelling. Her body was heavy, but she seemed all right except for the terrible look in her eyes. She frightened me every time I looked at her. I couldn't quite figure out whether it was longing or fear in her eyes, but it made me feel badly.

Mania was as calm as Mother used to be. Always in control of all her senses. Always on guard, she never complained. She took everything in stride. I remember the day she was punished. She was sewing a skirt for the Devil. We were sitting in front of the barracks and didn't notice the "Uniform" walking by. Well, he noticed us and walked straight toward her.

"Du, Schwein, where did you get this? You stole it, didn't you?" he yelled, kicking her with his heavy boots. He pushed her into the barracks and told the Devil to punish her by standing her in the corner of the barracks all day on sharp stones. The Devil didn't utter a word even though the skirt was hers. She made Mania stand there all day, and we all had to march by and watch her suffer.

Never before had I felt so strongly that I wanted to strangle somebody. I tried to get out of the line as we marched by, but Pola was holding me tightly. She knew better. It was no use. I would only make things worse. As long as Mania was in the barracks, she was alive.

After her punishment, tired and hungry (for the soup was denied her too) she went to sleep quietly without a word. She never complained. Her feet were still pierced from those stones when she climbed into the familiar cattle car.

We all climbed in. Twenty women in each car. What a luxury—to occupy quarters with only twenty women! Very soon a cart came by, and each of us received a slice of bread and a piece of margarine. We ate greedily, devouring every bite. No bread ever tasted so good. Nothing, no nothing, I ate before the war or at any time after had a taste like that slice of bread with margarine. And to add to our meager contentment, a large kettle of water was placed in our car as well!

The sun was setting when the door of our wagon was closed tightly, the train started to move: at first slowly, then faster and faster. Our hearts were pounding, stronger and stronger, for we were leaving the gas chambers of Auschwitz.

33 The wheels of the train were turning and so were the thoughts in our minds. We didn't speak, however. The silence that prevailed was a dead silence. No one dared to speak for fear something might happen and the bubble would burst. For we believed that we were living in a bubble, and as long as we were enclosed, we were alive.

The words of someone I had read were vivid in my mind:

> For there is one belief, one faith, and that is man's glory, his triumph, his immortality—and that is his belief in Life.

> Man loves life, hates death, and because of this he is great. He is glorious, he is beautiful. His beauty is everlasting. He lives in fear, in toil, in agony, and in unending tumult, but if the blood foamed bubbling from his wounded lungs at every breath he drew, he would still love life more dearly than an end of breathing.

> Dying, his eyes burn beautifully, and the hunger shines more fiercely in them [how true of Julek, I thought]. He has endured all the hard and purposeless suffering, and still he wants to live.

We did want to live, that we knew.

When the train stopped, we were allowed to get out. Surrounded by the dark, cold night, we walked one by one, under guard to take care of our physical needs. One by one we walked in again. How strange there was no desire to escape. No desire and no strength. Our bodies were tired and so were our minds. How far could I have run before the bullet hit me? I knew I couldn't run away and so did the others. This was a good place to rest our bodies and minds. Stretched out on the floor of the freight car, we slept close to one another. Twenty young bodies, covered in blue-and-white stripes all around. Shiny scalps, long noses, but no insides.

The bodies felt empty. There was nothing left inside. No feelings, no desires, not even tears. I looked at each of my

146

companions separately. Mania, Pola, Anna, Gienia, Tola, Lola and the others. They had all lost their dear ones. They had all lost their parents, their brothers and sisters. They had also thoroughly absorbed the smell of burning corpses. They all had the stamp of the whip on their bodies in one way or another, and yet they had no feelings. No one cried, not even Anna. My little Anna. How she must have suffered the loss of our mother.

I couldn't quite understand what was happening to us: how this transformation into something different from a human being had taken place, and how strangely we were taking it. There was no fighting against it, no arguments. The Germans were carrying out their plans, and no one objected.

"Kill all the Jews," was their cry. And they killed all the Jews. Whether they burned them in crematoria or took them away in cattle trains to work in Germany, it was all the same. We were just as dead as the others; the only difference was that we were still breathing. "And where there is life, there is hope," I remembered my mother used to say.

I remembered so well once when she was sick, very sick. Father came into our bedroom: "Ruth, Mania, wake up. I have to take Mother to the hospital. You watch the babies," he whispered.

I wiped my eyes in the kitchen and went to Mother's side. "Oh, Mother, dear Mother," I kissed her arm, but she could hardly see me. She had a high fever. I could see the tears rolling down her cheeks as she whispered to me: "Don't worry, my angel, where there is life there is hope. I'll be back."

The ambulance took her away; what an emptiness I felt then. Mother, my dear mother was gone. She was operated on the next morning, and the reports showed improvement from day to day. When she came home, we had a big "Welcome" sign on our doors. The sun was shining again, and my insides felt good and warm.

But this time it was different. This time she wasn't going to come back. How was I going to go on living? As I looked at the others, I realized that we were four orphans among thousands of orphans. Most of our parents were gone.

My thoughts were gone soon, too, because the rolling wheels of the train had put me to sleep. We were all sleeping. I didn't know for how long.

147

When I woke up, the train was at a stop. Soon we heard a whistle blow. At the sound of it, all the girls suddenly stood up. We realized how ridiculous this was and started to laugh; for there was no one on the train with us, and the doors were tightly locked. It crossed my mind that we had been taken back to Auschwitz. Mania must have had the same thoughts for she moved closer to me. "Ruth," she whispered fearfully.

"What are you thinking, Mania?" Pola asked with a wild look in her eyes.

"Nothing, really nothing," Mania answered quickly.

Suddenly the door opened. For a while we couldn't see a thing, because our eyes were unaccustomed to light. A wave of cold air made us shiver for a moment. Then we heard the shifting engines in the station yard and a tolling of a bell in the distance.

We noticed a little station in the middle of nowhere. Then we saw a small village in the distance with several homes over which towered the church from which the sound of the morning bell was ringing through the air. The air was cold and brisk. The sun was coming out slowly, but majestically. We were free. For a split second we were a part of this universe. It could have been anywhere in the world. It could have been a village at home. A small village in Poland, and we were being transferred there to live. To live and to breathe. We were beginning to feel, feel and want, to wish to live and breathe this fresh air.

Standing there on the steps of that freight car, facing nature, that unbelievable miracle that I thought I'd never see again, I lifted my arms, leaned back against the door and I could feel again, drink the air as I longed to drink life, to see tomorrow's sunshine.

34 A hundred women in blue-and-white-striped uniforms climbed out of the boxcars, their eyes rolling around but faces tired and hard, trying to find out where they were.

My hand reached automatically up to my head to smooth down my hair but there was no hair, just short, harsh roots slowly coming in. How funny Pola looked; her hair was standing up like a porcupine's.

Anna was frightened. She looked smaller than she was as she climbed out of the train. Her face was as wrinkled as the face of an old woman, but her shrunken body gave her the appearance of a little girl, for she was not yet fifteen.

Mania reached for my hand, and quickly we formed a group of five, taking Gienia with us. Poor Gienia. I could hardly forget the moment we saw her in Auschwitz, with her long, curly black hair, dressed in lovely clothes. Now there was this horrible transformation, her scalp shaven to the skin. In her blue-and-white-striped uniform, Gienia looked like a sausage, long, skinny and curved.

We left the railway station and walked through open fields. Here and there we spotted a farmhouse. There was life on those farms; there were people, chickens, and cows. How content and comfortable the cows in the fields looked to us. They were fed and rested; we were hungry and tired. The people on those farms had been feeding the cows and the chickens. What if they knew we were starved; would they give us a piece of potato, a slice of bread, or even a glass of milk?

I had a feeling that I wouldn't know what to do with a glass of milk. I had forgotten the taste of it. It had been years since any of us had had a glass or even a drop of milk.

"Pola, wouldn't you like to change places with this black and white cow?" Anna asked, when we passed the farm.

"Oh, no, not now. You don't know what you are talking about," Gienia reprimanded her. "The captain who brought us here is a wonderful man. We worked for him before in Krakow, we know. He has sent people ahead to build a house for us, and they are all nice people. They are not SS men. We are going to have a picnic here," Gienia went on.

"I can imagine the picnic the Germans would give us," Pola mumbled under her breath.

"Just you wait and see," Gienia answered.

"There is no reason to argue. God knows we could use a little human treatment and a little food for that matter, but we shall see the palaces soon," I said.

Most of us walked in silence. Some were praying and hoping. Some were still overpowered with the tragedies they had left behind in Auschwitz; they walked quietly with their heads down.

The guards were few and old. Their guns over their shoulders, they marched alongside us in silence. Here and there a human being stared at us through the window of his house, or from the back of it, as if frightened to face us or frightened of us.

Close to a barn stood a woman holding her two children close to her skirts; their big eyes looked at me with fear. A smile curved my lips, but the children only hid their faces in their mother's skirts.

My heart tightened, my lips opened, for in that split second, I wished I could say, Mother, Mother, where are you now? How I long to be near you, you will never know. How I need to be near you for just one breath, for just one second of your warmth, your love, your understanding. How I need to belong to someone, nobody will ever know.

I knew, though, that I had to be strong, for I was the oldest and my sisters needed me. I could never despair because that would mean the end of us all. I must breathe hope into their lungs. I must feed love into their hearts, for only then could we survive.

I squeezed Anna's hand just as the column was brought to a stop. In front of us, in place of a palace, were three wooden shacks. The shacks had ceilings and walls, but the builders had forgotten to put in a floor. Each of us was given a bundle of straw upon arrival to use as a bed. The barracks we were to live in were long but narrow. We were to sleep on each side of the wall, our feet just about reaching the other girl's. The five of us put our bundles of straw close to one another. The first night the straw felt good and clean, but in no time at all, it disappeared below the surface of the wet ground under it. The barracks had been built in a hurry, and as it was the rainy season, the ground was soaking wet. Even though the walls and the ceiling were there, the lack of heat didn't allow the ground to dry even a little, and one straw after another disappeared to mix with the earth. The good earth provided a wet, cold, uncomfortable bed for all of us.

Our barrack was connected with another one of the same size, but in the middle was a small room for the doctor who was to take care of our aches and pains. The doctor was a woman and she was from Krakow, too. She was in her forties, but having been through a few concentration camps already she looked at least eighty to me. She had been ordered to fight diseases in this camp, but there was absolutely no means, no medication, not even anything as simple as a bandage. Her diploma was supposed to be enough to take care of us and fight off whatever disease we contracted.

She had a little room, with one bed and a stove, a great luxury. On the other side of her room was the second barrack. Strangely enough, the girls who occupied it formed a separate group. They were all from the city of Radom, or from its vicinity. They called themselves Radomianki, Girls from Radom.

I have used the term "girls" to describe these women, but the fact is that among these girls were a few who were well into their forties and were mothers to girls our age. Separated from their dear ones and miraculously having survived Auschwitz, or other concentration camps, they had to act like girls. They mixed well with all of us; they did the same hard work we did and suffered as much from the hardships. Every now and then one of us would become attached to one of them and surround her with attention and respect. A friendship would develop, a mutual dependency, and motherhood would bloom. Everybody was hungry for love.

The ground was lightly frozen and the air cold as we walked to work the next morning. Even though the guards were watching us, we felt free. We walked through a little village where we saw houses here and there. There were open fields as far as we could see and fresh air. How we all longed to breath this fresh air; there was no smell of burned bodies in it. And to think that I had almost believed there was no other air but the polluted, smelling air of Auschwitz. I could hardly believe that I had come out of there; it didn't seem possible that anyone of us would ever come out of that hell.

"One day we shall just walk away and walk for days and nights, for we shall be free. Can't you see?" Anna asked.

"Sure, I can see," Pola murmured. "In the first place, you are forgetting that we are somewhere in Germany. Who knows where? In the second place, the Germans are all the same. They have one purpose—to kill all the Jews. Do you think for a moment that one of them would open the door for us, or give us food? Didn't you see how they ran when they saw us? They think we are some kind of animal, a species they have never seen before. No wonder. Whoever saw women without hair? Don't think you can fly. You are a Jewish bird, and a Jewish bird has no place to fly."

"All right, so I shall not fly, but I got out of Auschwitz, and that is something," Anna snapped.

We certainly came out of Auschwitz. And yet there was a burning wound inside of us that was Auschwitz. It burned constantly like the flame that had consumed the bodies of our beloved mother, little Mojshele, Mrs. B. my "future mother-in-law," many, many relatives and friends. Auschwitz left a mark outside, too, after all what is a woman without her glory on her head, without hair? A woman who doesn't menstruate? We had lost our dignity in Auschwitz. We had no clothes that looked feminine and no desire to act like ladies. Even more than all that, we had learned to live with death, and the strong drive for survival penetrated all of us.

We each received a slice of bread that morning, and I watched the women eat it, their eyes rolling wildly, looking at it, their tongues munching the bread, holding it in their mouths for a long period, as if to relish the taste. Animal looks and movements marked all of us. All of us but Mania. She had that calm look and movement, self-control—she was still human.

After a long march, we came to a railway station. We were told that our job was to load the train with Nachrichten Gerete. All sorts of equipment for the army produced in this village were to be loaded and reloaded by us, one hundred women. Equipment to build telephone connections, telephone poles, and the connecting parts for telephone and telegraph service. Two of us had to carry one telephone pole. (Sometimes I look at the telephone poles near my home and wonder how in the world it was possible for two girls, hungry, tired, exhausted by war, to carry a telephone pole on their shoulders, that was at least forty feet long and two feet wide.) But I remember carrying one for many a day. The flesh of my shoulder was soon ripped, my back bent from its heavy load, but I had no choice. If we didn't move fast enough, the guards quickly landed a few lashes on our backs, and the flesh opened there too. Many times, infection plagued our raw bodies, but this too couldn't stop us, for we had to produce, come day, come night, come rain or snow.

Yet there was something light about this work, about the whole atmosphere in this camp. Mainly, I think, it was the idea that we had come out of Auschwitz and, therefore, we would live. When we returned to our barracks, tired, hungry, and cold, we went on and on building our hopes for the future. We imagined that the captain who supposedly had gotten us out of Auschwitz was a Prophet, the Messiah we all waited for. Or another time he was an English spy, who had received an order to save the one hundred women, and any time, any day, the English would drop with their parachutes and take us all to safety. Some other times, he was just an angel.

Soon, though, our angel turned into a devil. Our rations were cut down, our work was increased. Disease began to spread. Our poor doctor tried to help, but she had no ways or means. In the meantime, a heavy winter came upon us.

"The Germans are losing the war and they take it out on us," Gienia whispered.

"How do you know?" I asked.

"One of the soldiers told me," she motioned toward a young officer who was watching us.

The next morning I tried to find work near where the officer stood. The instruments we were loading were extremely heavy. I had developed an infection in my mouth, and blood was pouring out all the time. It weakened me considerably, and I struggled with the heavy box, unable to lift it. Suddenly someone's hand came from the other side and lifted it for me. I looked up and two sad eyes looked at me. Quickly, I reached for my head to smooth my hair, but there was hardly any to smooth; in front I had a little curl. A man was looking at me. I dropped my eyes quickly for fear I had done something wrong; after all, he was a German guard.

During the day, he seemed to follow me every now and then.

"Du," he whispered, "you can lift this box much easier if you use your intelligence instead of your strength, which you don't have." He showed me that there was another way of lifting the box. When I put my hand on the box, he put his hand on mine. I removed it in panic. But slowly he did it again, and the box went up into the freight car without too much strain!

Objects became lighter and easier to lift. I still don't know whether there is such a theory. I do know that it helped me. I shall probably never know how I did it, but I did. My work became much easier, considerably easier.

One morning, the officer slipped a slice of bread, or rather a good chunk of bread near us. The next day a little sugar. We all shared the extra food with great delight. I, myself, tried to figure out what was happening. Here was a German officer trying to help me. Why? Who was he? My imagination started working again. God had sent him—another angel. We needed so many angels. When one day he took my hand in his, making sure that nobody saw, not even my fellow prisoners, I knew he was a man. He was a man, but he was a German. Could it be? Was it possible? Could there be a German with feelings and sympathy for a Jewish girl? Going to work every day became easier, and I looked forward to seeing him and having his eyes on me every now and then.

"The war will be over soon, for you too," he would whisper. "You will soon be free. Do not despair; just hold out a little longer." The girls were envious of my friend but always eager to find out what news he brought. He was our contact with the outside world. He gave us hope. And to me it was a new, wonderful feeling awakening again. A man looked at me! I was still a girl! Mania had managed to make me a little square to cover my head so that only my lock of hair showed, and some days when the officer looked at me and smiled, I felt beautiful, I felt young, and I had hopes again.

35 The temperature must have been well below zero one day when we came to work. My eyes kept wandering all around for my benefactor, but he was nowhere in sight. He was gone; I never even knew his name.

It had been a long, long day at work, and when we returned to the barracks, the snow was falling. It was a welcome sight these days, for there was no water; the pipes had frozen and the snow was refreshing to our dry tongues. It was wonderful also for washing. When we got up in the morning half-frozen, we would rub the snow all over our bodies; the lack of water and soap could be felt already. Our bodies were covered with abscesses of all kinds; open wounds that discharged pus. Our poor doctor couldn't help us, for she had no supplies whatsoever. Finally one day, she, too, became ill. She occupied the little room next to our barrack and I often went to talk to her. She was making plans for her future, telling me how she hoped to open an office in Krakow. She even had the home planned for it already. Together we were decorating her office in our minds and talking about the wonderful times long past. One night she, too, was removed; where and how nobody knew.

We awoke every morning with the fear that someone else would be sick and unable to work. Mania suffered from the cold more than any of us. Poor Mania, she could take hunger, but she couldn't take the cold. In the meantime, the work was getting harder; the days were shorter, and more and more wagons had to be loaded. The Germans, in a frenzy, were beating anyone who came under their whips. They pushed harder and harder. But nothing would help, for our bodies were tired, undernourished, and ill.

Pola was having nightmares, and Anna stayed awake at night for fear she would freeze if she fell asleep. We stayed up talking and wondering what was going on with the population of our nearby village. Didn't they see what was happening to us? They saw us going to work and working like horses, in cold and hunger. Many a time one of us whispered to them: "Water, bread; we are hungry," but they just turned away. They didn't want to hear or see.

We heard bells ringing clear and loud. We saw the people of Gundelsdorf walk to church on Christmas morning. We went to work. There were only a few guards, for the others had a day off for Christmas. We had to load telephone poles on the freight cars. On that Christmas morning, they seemed exceptionally heavy. Pola and I picked the longest one there was, I guess. The guard with his whip stood over us, and as soon as we had the pole on our shoulders, he told us to run with it. His whip hit my legs, I tripped, and the pole knocked me down; the guard's whip still lashed at me. I was lying on the ground unconscious. The last thing I remembered was the sight of the pole over my eyes. I was sure it would break my head in half.

When I came to, I was in my barrack and Pola was sitting next to me. My head was bandaged with sheets, my legs too. I felt a terrible pain, almost unbearable, and I couldn't move. My whole body hurt. I looked around but didn't really see. I knew Pola was with me, for she kept repeating, "I am sorry, I am sorry. I didn't mean to let it go." Poor girl, she never had a chance; how could she hold that monster of a pole on her shoulder by herself?

"He had to whip you even so, that dirty swine. I'll kill him," Pola continued. I put my hand over hers, but even my hand hurt. The bells kept ringing in my head.

"It's Christmas, you know. It's Christmas. Maybe they will——" Pola began. I nodded my head. I wanted her to continue so much. Perhaps now, perhaps she will say something nice, perhaps now she will have a little hope, a tiny little spark, if only for me. But she just looked at me.

The others came from work. They all dropped on their bunks. Before night came, I lifted my head a little but was relieved to go to sleep again.

Christmas came and passed, and New Year's came, but the people of Gundelsdorf didn't see or hear anything. They were cuddled in their warm homes and filling their stomachs with delicious warm food. They wined and dined, while one hundred women were dying of starvation, cold, and hard labor right under their noses.

The hope we had when we first came to Gundelsdorf! A village full of human beings with families, with children of their own. A village of people and not soldiers—and in the midst of this village, a tragedy beyond description happening right under the eyes of these human beings—celebrating Christmas and offering prayers to God. Could this make any sense to anyone? It didn't to me. Day by day, the hope we had was vanishing.

At the end of January, a transport of one hundred men was brought into our camp. A new barrack was built for them. The men were mostly Greek, some Hungarian. They didn't have a chance to go through channels, as we had, that is, Auschwitz and other concentration camps; they were taken directly out of their warm, comfortable homes into the cold, unbearable weather and bare barracks of Gundelsdorf.

For food they were given a bowl of water with scarcely a pea swimming in it. When they went to work the first day, they couldn't believe that we women had done this job for months. Their backs broke under the heavy loads. Every time they bent, the whips rested on their backs. In a few days, they all looked like animals, their eyes wild, their mouths moving, and their hands always stretched out for food.

The Germans even brought a doctor with them, but he too could not help anyone. He had no supplies, only his diploma, which couldn't be much help under these unprecedented conditions.

The doctor was from Poland, and we all jumped at him trying to find out where he had been before and who of our families or friends he could have seen. This was the first camp he had come to as he had been hiding in a Polish home until now. Somebody had revealed his hiding place. Fortunately for him, however, he was not shot immediately but sent to this camp. Now he wondered whether he was fortunate indeed!

One day he called me to his barrack. The Greeks were dying like flies. They couldn't take the hunger and the cold. When I walked in, he showed me a dead body lying on the bunk. He pointed to its hands, but I couldn't understand what he meant.

"Can't you see?" he yelled. "They have bitten off the flesh from its bones! They are crazy, stark mad! They are going to get typhus. What am I to do?"

I froze. I couldn't utter a word. When I gathered my strength again, I ran. I ran to my barrack and dropped on my straw bed, crying violently. "Ruth, Ruth," I heard my sisters calling, but I didn't care. I didn't even care about them anymore. I just wanted to die. Mania pushed a piece of bread into my mouth, but I couldn't swallow it. The sight of men eating their own flesh remained in my mind.

For the next few days, I went to work like a robot. Blood was gushing from my mouth and I was getting weaker every day.

In the meantime, Mania was working out a scheme that would help her to get out of the cold and help us to survive, which, at the moment, seemed impossible to accomplish. She had managed to tell one officer that she could sew. She could sew anything his family needed. He had a wife and four children with him in this godforsaken place, and the prospect looked good to him. Mania was able to work in a separate room attached to his house.

She was escorted by the guard to his place and back. The room was warm. What a relief for Mania's stiff limbs. And she received half a loaf of bread every day. We began to live again. With the extra bread, we could get up in the morning. One night, we decided to leave a quarter of the bread for morning and hide it under our heads. When we woke up in the morning, the bread was gone.

Pola yelled and cried and suspected everyone in our barrack. A fight started; the girls were pulling at each other, grabbing at each other's clothes, pulling what little hair there was. A mass of wild bodies tumbled to the floor. Poor Pola was on the bottom of it. Anna, Mania, and I tried to separate them all, and finally, exhausted, ashamed, and tired, they stopped.

I had a feeling I knew who could have taken the bread; but I couldn't really be too harsh with her, for she was hungry too. Every now and then I pushed a piece of bread in her direction.

One day Mania came from work and told me that she had told the officer about my mouth bleeding constantly, and he had promised her he would take me to a doctor. I was allowed to go to the railway station after we had finished work in order to wash. What a relief to have real, running water. I scrubbed and washed, for I was going to see a doctor.

The next morning, I was picked up in a truck. My eyes had

to be covered with a scarf. I wasn't supposed to see or speak all through the trip. In front was the officer, in back, a guard, and in the middle me, little me, with eyes tight, my mouth shut. What were they afraid of?

I was going on a trip. I imagined that I was in a beautiful yellow limousine going home with my beloved. He was holding my hand and telling me how much he loved me. He was going to tell my parents that he wanted to marry me. I was blushing. I could see my mother, rushing, fixing, cooking, preparing a fabulous meal. Was it going to be a chicken or maybe a duck? Her oldest daughter was coming home with her fiancé. I could just see father beaming. He was so proud of his daughter. His eye twitched, he was telling Mojshele that Ruth was coming home. He was telling Anna to behave and be sweet. Pola and Mania were scheming already how to play tricks on Ruth's fiancé.

Suddenly the jeep came to a stop. I was led somewhere; the guard was holding my hand. How I wished I could give him something—some disease. My eyes were uncovered just before I walked into a room that was like a waiting room in any hospital.

I was brought into a dentist's office. Frightened, I sat there, forbidden to talk. After my officer explained something in German, the dentist went to work, and before I knew it, I was five teeth poorer. What did my poor teeth have to do with the bleeding? I couldn't imagine. All I could see was more blood gushing from my mouth. He handed me something to take with me for rinsing my mouth, and after I left his office, my eyes were blindfolded again and I was taken back to the camp.

Our camp doctor was waiting to hear where I was and what had happened. He, too, was hoping that maybe now the Germans were getting softer, for his men really needed help. Every time someone died, the others wouldn't let the body be removed, for at night they would feast on the flesh.

My sisters greeted me with relief as I returned to the barrack. The air was filled with excitement, for while I was gone, they had learned that a sewing factory in the vicinity needed twenty girls. Everyone wanted to go. This was an opportunity to stay under a roof and perhaps even get a little food. By a lucky coincidence, the four of us were among the twenty chosen. I had never before sewn on a sewing machine, and an electric one at that.

"Mania," I whispered at night. "What am I going to do?" In a determined tone, she snapped: "You are going to sew!"

"But how?"

All through the night, I prayed. I prayed that God would help me, would enlighten me, would show me the way; I had to be with my sisters.

It was a long march to the factory on that February morning in 1945.

"You thread the needle, first here, then there. Then you put your foot on the pedal, pull out the thread from underneath," Mania repeatedly explained all the way to the factory, showing all the motions, as if the machine were in front of me. She did all this in a muffled voice, not daring to reveal even in front of the other girls, that I couldn't sew. We arrived at the factory and entered a long room with machines standing in two rows. The guards stayed outside, while inside there was just one German supervisor. He distributed yarn, and then pieces of rubber, explaining that we were to sew aprons for the German soldiers.

I sat next to Mania. At a command all the machines started; *mine wouldn't start.* I had put the yarn in wrong. Mania quickly bent over my machine and started it for me. Oh, God, did I pray that morning. My machine soon started its bzzzzz . . . The rubber was difficult to sew on, but my machine moved, moved one way and then another. I looked at Mania and followed what she did. Pretty soon the noise stopped. One apron was ready. Mine, too! Since I was first in the row, the guard picked mine up. I trembled. This apron meant life or death for me, I knew.

"Here, look here. That is good, that is the way it has to be done," the German supervisor emphasized.

"Adon Olam," was all I could say.

By the end of the day, my energy was completely exhausted, but several aprons still had to be made. When the supervisor wasn't looking, I slipped a few to Mania and she finished them for me. I knew, however, that I couldn't continue to do that because every day a certain number had to be finished by each of us.

Rozia was helping the supervisor cut the aprons for us with an electric fabric cutter. I watched her every now and then with envy. That was something I could do; it demanded a little concentration, but no special skill. I could learn to do it, but in the meantime, what about Rozia?

On Monday when we all came to work, Rozia had a bandage on her foot. She couldn't stand on her feet and asked the supervisor if she could sew for a couple of days until her abscess opened up. I jumped to my feet!

"Could I try to cut?" I begged.

"Well, it is a responsibility; one wrong move and all the material is wasted. We cannot afford to waste any material," the German snarled at me. I returned to my machine. Later in the afternoon, however, the German called me, put the cutter in my hand, and there I was for better or for worse.

The cutter and I fell in love at first sight. I could move it easily and swiftly. Within one week, I had developed such speed that my supervisor said he would make a bet with me. If I could cut faster than he, I would get a loaf of bread. I couldn't believe it. I felt light and happy; I almost flew over the table and over the material. Faster and faster, for I knew that at the end there would be a loaf of bread.

I won! A whole loaf of bread in a paper bag was handed to me on the way home. A whole loaf of bread! It was such a temptation to cut it into four pieces and be full for once. But after talking it over, we decided that we should share it with everyone. Twenty slices of bread; each of us ate the bread quickly for fear it would disappear.

When we returned to the barracks that evening, there was no one there. The barrack was empty. We found our places and lay awake afraid to utter a word, waiting for our friends to come back. At first, we thought they were working late. We waited and waited, but they never came back.

The night was long and terribly dark; we were frightened.

When the whistle blew, we jumped to our feet unaware of what time it was. Through the louvers we could see it was daylight.

We went outside and washed our faces in the snow, and not seeing any movement, we walked quietly into the next barrack. There was no one there.

I ran over to the men's barrack, but there was no one there, either. Not even a clue as to what might have happened to our friends and neighbors. Many thoughts went through our minds, but very soon our own destiny was at stake again.

36 The four of us were sitting on our freezing bed and making some plans. Early that morning we had heard the roaring of the planes and, of course, we believed they must be American planes. They were near. Pretty soon they would bomb all the city around us; then our guards would get frightened and run for their lives, and the twenty of us would run for our lives.

"You know, I am so used to this life under guard, the lovely straw under my back, and the bowl of soup or slice of bread every day, that I wouldn't know what to do with my freedom," Anna said.

Mania added: "I would be surprised if you even remembered what freedom was all about. After all, you've spent half of your lifetime in here."

"Don't! Let her dream. We are not free yet. Leave it to the Germans. They will come up with something before the war is over," Pola argued.

"Pola, Pola," I said. "Must you always sound so gloomy?"

"You not only act but sound like Mother already. P-o-la, P-o-la, must you always sound so gloomy?" Pola repeated.

At this, Anna sighed, "How I wish Mother were here now."

"And Father, and Mojshele," Mania added quietly.

Silence again; it seemed as though we had no right to even mention their names aloud.

Another loud roar in the skies. We ran outside but they had gone already.

Only more snow had covered the ground; and when the guard blew his whistle, the twenty of us automatically moved, marching to work again. My mouth had gotten a little better in the last several weeks. Perhaps being inside and having a little more bread here and there had helped.

Each night we returned to the barracks and sat and hoped that the Americans would come down out of the skies, take all the guards prisoners and allow us our freedom. No matter what happened, no matter who won the war ultimately, it was absolutely immaterial. The thing that counted was that the twenty of us would be taken away from this freezing hell and into a warm home, wherever it might be, even in America which seemed so distant to us.

On 20 March 1945, an open truck came to pick us up. For a moment, we thought our dreams had come true; but it was Pola who quickly shook us from our illusions.

"You idiots! What are you rejoicing about?" she almost yelled. "Don't you remember how they took Mojshele and all the others? We are going on a trip all right. What are you taking with you? We won't need anything where we're going," she cried.

The whistle blew and the guard told us to get our belongings and climb onto the truck. We all huddled together, for it was a very clear, freezing morning, well below zero. We warmed ourselves with our bodies and our breath. The wind was blowing, and it seemed after a while that all of us would just die of cold, quietly without a word. No one spoke. The skies were blue above us.

I looked up into the blue and silver early dawn air and prayed. I prayed for the last time as I knew I couldn't survive this trip much longer, and yet there was no bitterness in my prayer. I prayed with my mind, yet my heart was somehow fortified and was at peace. There was no fear in my heart. It was strange. Was it peace because I was going to live, or peace because I was going to die? If I were to die, who would look after my sisters? Poor Pola, she grew more bitter every day, and her eyes, her eyes looked wild like a little animal's—starved, cold and bitter. And Mania, Mania who could never stand the cold; how could she possibly survive this trip? I didn't even want to think of little Anna, whose eyes were opening and closing from exhaustion, yet she was afraid to fall asleep. I finished my prayers for all of them and sat waiting.

Finally the truck came to a stop in the grey-green winter snow. We entered the gate of a camp. We were counted and recounted again. When we had gotten off the truck, we could hardly stand on our frozen feet. The whole world seemed to be dominated by the cold glow of the winter sun. Barely noticing anything, a few tumbled to the ground. Anna held onto me tightly.

164

A group of women took charge of us. Well, the Germans were running out of men, we hoped. We were taken into a barrack where two hundred women were sleeping. There was a completely different atmosphere here, and the place itself was entirely different from any concentration camp we had seen before, but we didn't know why. First, we realized that the bunks which were three stories high were single. That frightened me a little, for I always liked to have my sisters near me. But this place was somehow different. The women appeared different too. Some looked like men, and some looked like women. The most important discovery, however, was that none of these inmates was Jewish.

They all surrounded us asking out of curiosity where we had come from, why had we been arrested. When we explained that we were there because we were Jewish, they couldn't understand and insisted that we must have done something against the law, for this particular camp was for criminals only.

One heavy woman told us that she had spent twenty years in this rot because she had killed her husband. Another one had taken part in a robbery and had been in the camp for a decade. There was a group of so-called politicals. They were from Poland. They had participated in the Warsaw underground, and the Germans had caught them and imprisoned them. Another group that stuck together were the prostitutes. They had found a place in jail, too. But the twenty of us, young girls who had never hurt a fly? Why should we suffer here, they asked.

Zwodau was such a strange world to us. It could have been another planet. The occupants were different from any people we had ever known. The language they used was not familiar to us at all. The morals and the behavior of the prisoners was very strange indeed. At first, it was funny to see the girls with the boyish haircuts, with pants and flat-looking chests. We thought that boredom had brought them to this. After all, one might try anything after being imprisoned for years. But we discovered very soon that these people weren't playing games.

At night the barracks came alive with one woman seeking another. We soon realized why the beds were single, but even that didn't stop them. Discomfort didn't mean anything; they managed. I stayed awake many a night afraid that someone might come and attack one of us. I wanted so much to protect Anna from all that; from the language they used, from discovery of what these women were doing. I, myself, had a hard time realizing what it was all about, never mind Anna, who was only fifteen at the time.

Mrs. Biskupska, who had a bed next to mine, explained all the maneuvers to me and warned me that if I remained indifferent, they would leave me alone. Anyhow, the war would be over soon, she always said. She was one of the politicals and believed that the Germans were losing the war and that any day it would be over. Mrs. Biskupska knew that the Americans were in the war now, that the German invasion of Russia had been a complete fiasco, and that the Russians were marching on the retreating Germans towards Poland and Germany. It was good to listen to her. Hope flickered in our hearts even though our morale was really low.

I became very gloomy at times, and then it was one or another of my sisters who had a spark of hope, and always carried it to all four of us. It was enough for one to say something good, and we all responded to it, even Pola sometimes.

Soon, we learned something else about Zwodau. There were two thousand women, and nearly all the food was running out. At first, we received a slice of bread in the morning and a pot of cold black liquid that looked like coffee. In the evening, we each were given a bowl of soup. Very soon, the bread disappeared, and after that, we had only the bowl of soup, once a day, that is, if we were lucky. All day long, we waited for the soup. We rushed to get into line. If we got lucky in front then we ended up with a bowl of warm water with nothing in it. The next time, we tried to stand at the end of the line; perhaps the soup would be thickest there. But by the time our turn came, there was no soup left. The supervisor rolled the barrel over; we reached for it with our hands; we tried to find something there, some little piece of potato, anything to stop our hunger. We licked our fingers, but there was nothing there. Of course, when it was one only of the four of us who managed to receive some morsel, we would share whatever we had with each other. But what of those others?

Hunger pains kept us awake at night; and in the morning, when the whistle blew and we had to go to the factory to work, we rolled off our beds and went to work automatically. Day by day, we were getting weaker. Something I had never experienced before was becoming clear to me now. How did people die of starvation? How did it feel, and how could one possibly live without food?

Was it just a physical agony or did the body and soul die together? I knew now that it was something nobody could understand without experiencing fully to comprehend the anguish one is subjected to. The death which comes by starvation is a prolonged death of unutterable torment. There were days when Anna awoke in the morning and tried to get up, but couldn't. Her frail young body was unwilling to bend to more torture from the hunger pains cramping and turning her stomach and intestines. She could not lift herself off the hard, cold, wooden board to get up, to walk, to stand in the Appellplatz, day in and day out, her young face like the dried-up remains of autumn leaves.

Then there was the frantic look in Pola's eyes when her mouth was dry and her tongue wouldn't produce any saliva to swallow. With the terrible dryness of mouth and body, for there is no water to satisfy the thirst, or the unbearable hunger, the body becomes shrunken, the voice feeble and remote.

And how many times did Mania disappear from our sight so we couldn't see her suffer? She would rather die than have us see her suffer. And I, myself, half-crazed with the pain of headaches, day after day, was so dizzy that I didn't see where I was going. Poor Anna, pretended she was holding onto me, but she knew very well that she was helping me to walk, for the pain in my head completely oppressed my senses.

Yes, starvation is another cruel way of dying; the body dies, inch by inch, day by day, and yet one lives.

How did we live through this death? Was it because we were young, or was it because we were determined to survive? Was it simply a miracle? To the four of us it was all these things and even more. It was a feeling of togetherness, of belonging, and of the great love we had for each other, and an even greater love of life.

It was this desire to live and the love of life that helped us to survive Zwodau, for Zwodau wasn't just another concentration camp. It was a whole new experience, a world strange to us. Although we remained there for only a few weeks, it seemed

167

like an eternity. We heard rumors that the work at the factory was coming to an end. The Americans were coming. The attitude of the people who worked with us in this airplane factory had changed a little, and one or the other would slip a slice of bread to us, when the guards weren't looking. We all shared everything, and many times the slice of bread amounted to a crumb for each. But we were a small island of people in this strange world in Zwodau, and we knew we had to stick together. The twenty of us had been together for quite a while now, and our sufferings and our common goal had brought us closer to each other than any family ties could have.

The 15th of April—my birthday. The sun was shining when I woke to the sound of a whisper, "Happy Birthday to you," from Anna. Pola handed me a slice of bread, a whole slice of bread. The most wonderful gift I have ever received for my birthday for as long as I live. All the girls decided that I must eat the whole slice. I couldn't even swallow it at first, but I munched it all, and felt sudden strength coming into me. It seemed that the whole world looked brighter. I wasn't hungry for this one moment. I was happy!

The American artillery sounded louder and louder. The "political" told us that the Americans were fifteen miles away, but it sounded even closer, especially in the quiet of the night. We didn't go to work any more, and it was like a big holiday that day, because it was my birthday, and because we expected the war to end just then. Year after year, I had hoped that the war would end on my birthday, and now it seemed that it definitely would. The Americans were going to march into the camp, and we would all run into their arms. But it was only my elevated spirits and the slice of bread that had made me feel so good.

Freedom was such a long way off.

37

It was 18 April 1945.

It rained most of the day. We all sat on our bunks reminiscing and making plans for the future. The Americans were coming. Were they all as glamorous as the movie stars? Were they all rich? Would they bring with them the food and fruit we used to dream about? An orange? A banana? Or maybe a lemon, full of sour, vitamin-filled juice—a fruit we couldn't even afford to buy when we lived at home. I remembered when I went to school in Krakow, and Father would come to visit me, he would always buy one orange for me and one for Grandmother. I could smell and taste the juicy, sweet meat of that heavenly fruit. But in America, in America, these fruits grew on trees, and in America people had everything.

I had studied English for quite a few years before the war began and tried to remember some of the words now, but I hardly dared to say them aloud, not even in front of my sisters. Someone might overhear me and I could be tried for spying. Tried, did I say? Hanged was more like it.

It was late in the evening when the "cemetery commando" returned. They went to work every day and dug graves, for every day somebody died in this camp of two thousand. Today, it was different, however, they told us. They had had to dig all day—a sort of mass grave. They were wet and tired. Night found all of us asleep on 18 April 1945.

At 11:00 P.M. the woman Blockelteste woke me and the other nineteen girls and told us to come outside just with our nightgowns on, nothing else; it would just be for a moment. We rolled out of our beds and stood in the cold of the night. It was quiet, very dark, and very quiet. The twenty of us stood there, and in seconds several men and women guards surrounded us, pointing their guns at us.

The mass grave crossed my mind. But there was no time to think. Anna, Pola, Mania, Gienia, and I formed the first five. We followed the guards towards the gate. I looked at one SS woman questioningly, and she looked up at the skies. That was her answer. No one uttered a word. Even the guards were unusually quiet, no whistles, no orders.

We left the gate. The thought of freedom crossed my mind, but there was no time to make an escape. We were told to move faster, faster. Running in the dark, in the cold, in the quiet of the night. Where were we going? The question crossed my mind. We were inside a wall. A cemetery wall. We were standing around a big hole. That is what the cemetery commando had been digging all day. We knew now.

A mass grave for whom? For us? Twenty Jewish girls from fourteen to twenty-four. Enemies of the German Reich who will be shot to death on this day of 18 April 1945, and buried in this unknown cemetery where no one will ever be able to find them. But why, why now, when the Americans were only a few miles away. Tears were rolling down our cheeks, and Janka broke into spasmodic sobs. "Mother, Mother, please help me."

"I shall never see my parents again," another girl cried.

Tola begged: "Girls, girls, let's die with honor; let's not show them we are weak."

"Die with honor," Pola returned. "For what? What have we done to anybody? Why, why?" she cried. But Anna could only moan in a low voice, "I'll never eat a hot potato again." Poor Anna, how hungry she must have been. I'll never forget her last wish before she was to be shot. (To this day, whenever I cook potatoes, I dig into the pot for the one hot potato that she dreamed of on that cold, dark night in April.)

"Why don't they get it over with? What are they waiting for?" another girl cried. It seemed for a moment that everything was in utter confusion, even the guards seemed bewildered. They whispered among themselves as we stood there around the grave, surrounded by their guns. All the while, far in the distance we could hear the beautiful sounds of the American artillery.

I looked at my sisters and couldn't say anything. Could it be that only three days ago, on my birthday, our hopes had been so high, and freedom so near? What could we do now? Twenty young girls between the grave and the guns? If they would only get it over with. Oh, Lord, please help me. Let the first shot kill me instantly. I couldn't stand to see my sisters

170

being shot. I couldn't. Let it be me first. Will I have to jump into the hole while they shoot? Or——A tremendous roar came from nearby. For a moment it felt as though the ground was shaking beneath us. One girl cried:

"The Americans are coming!"

"Shma Israel," cried another.

"Don't you hear? The Americans are coming!" Gienia yelled to the guard. He hit her over the head with his gun and she lay sprawled on the ground, looking blankly around.

"If you shoot us, they will shoot you," I uttered to the SS woman next to me. And Mania quickly added: "If you save us, we shall tell the Americans and they will save you too."

The guards started talking to each other.

"If they don't want to shoot you," one SS woman pointed to the guards, "then I shall shoot all of you with this machine gun."

She was only a young girl. Her belly was big; she was expecting a baby. For the Führer no doubt. The Führer said to have babies; she had babies. The Führer said, shoot the Jews; she was going to shoot the Jews. How poisoned was this poor soul.

How could she give birth to a new life after she had killed twenty innocent young girls? It seemed like an eternity standing there waiting to be killed.

Suddenly, with quick movements, they told us to go back to camp. They chased us and we ran. We ran as fast as our feet would carry us. The gate opened and in the middle of that dark, cold night on 18 April 1945, we returned from our grave into the camp of Zwodau.

We were too frightened to think about what had happened. Nothing made any sense to us and nothing meant anything. The fact was that we were alive. Or were we? How much life was there left in us? We sat on our bunks waiting. Would they come back in the morning?

The two hundred women who had been sleeping all through it were now awake. They couldn't believe what had happened. One young Polish girl said to me: "I shall never believe in God if the Germans kill you twenty innocent girls." They all looked at us as though we were saints, something set apart, perhaps not even human.

And then something happened that I shall never forget as

171

long as I live. Mrs. Biskupska stood up on her bunk and said loudly: "Girls, we shall all say rosaries for these twenty young girls who were to be shot because of their belief in God."

Two hundred woman—the criminals, the politicals, the lesbians, the prostitutes—all of them stood on their bunks and recited the rosary. All of them united in prayer. It was like music, like a miracle, so unbelievable, and yet so true. Two hundred women of different nationalities, different religions, all prayed for us. We joined them in prayer and hoped that our prayers would be heard, that at last we should be free and that the Germans wouldn't come back for us that night or any other night.

We couldn't go back to sleep. Every noise, every sound we heard made us think they were coming back for us, but the morning found us alive after all.

We were destined to live and not to die. "Listen, girls," Anna called out softly to those who could hear: "When the war is over, let us all meet together so we can laugh about it and tell our children about it."

"Are you being ridiculous?" Pola asked.

"Of course not. I mean it, we must survive now, and in ten years, perhaps even sooner, we will all meet somewhere, somehow."

Anna's enthusiasm didn't convince us, but we needed something to strengthen our faith quickly.

"I think Anna's idea is wonderful," I said. "We will all meet in Krakow in the year—let's think—1955. If only the Americans would come now and save us all!"

38 The Americans didn't come that day; instead, a large transport of six hundred women from another camp stopped overnight at Zwodau. These women were all Jewish. Some of them had been with us in Plaszow. From them, we also learned that Plaszow had been liquidated, that everybody had been sent away to other concentration camps.

"What happened to the Jewish Police?" I asked Lola, whom I knew from Plaszow. "They were all shot to death," she answered.

"Did you say all of them?" I asked fearfully.

"Yes, and your almighty cousin Emil, too. He was shot at the end with the camp's elite. After all, he belonged to them, didn't he?" she asked.

I walked slowly to my bunk; my thoughts were with Emil. Yes, my dear sweet cousin Emil belonged to the elite. Tears rolled down my cheeks. My heart ached for this young boy who might have grown to be among the great, the cream of society, had it not been for this terrible, crippling war. He had simply been caught in the whirlpool and didn't know how to get out of it. Poor Emil died from a bullet on the grounds of Plaszow Concentration Camp with no one to bury him and no one to shed a tear. I would never see him again.

I lay awake all night, trying to understand what was really happening. Yesterday the twenty of us had been saved from an imminent death. How and why I couldn't possibly explain. One moment I knew we were all as good as dead, and the next moment our lives had been spared. My sisters were sleeping next to me, but I couldn't close my eyes. Was I afraid to sleep? What a silly thought. There was no fear in me; there were no feelings whatsoever, yet my heart was so heavy. Emil was dead. My dear edelweiss. It seemed like yesterday that we climbed the mountains in Grandmother's backyard in Sopotnia and picked the little flowers that would live forever; edelweiss, the little flowers that live forever.

But Emil was gone—young, ambitious, so anxious to grab all he could in his nineteen short years.

My little Mojshele, eleven years old, eleven short years. Not even enough time to learn about life.

And my dear mother—so young, so lovely, always cheerful, always seeing the world through pink glasses. She, too, had joined Mojshele. And what of Mrs. B.—a devoted mother and wife who, arriving at Auschwitz, had hoped to find her one and only son? She too had found death; now she would never see her son even if he were alive. In spite of the ashes that had been sent to her, and in spite of all the messages she had received that he was dead, she had gone on believing that he was alive. What if he really were alive? Would I ever see him? And if I did see him by some miraculous coincidence, would her wishes come true?

My dear, dear father. How I wished I knew where he was now. How I wished I could help him. For it was he who needed help. From the moment that Mojshele was taken away, his desire to live had left him. His hair had turned gray overnight, his face ashen. A woman from the newly arrived transport offered that he had probably been sent to Matthausen, because most of the men from Plaszow had been sent there. What was Matthausen? What did he have to do there? Did he have enough food to survive? Oh, Father, dear Father, please survive for our sake. If the four of us are meant to survive, what can we do without a mother or father?

What can we do? What can we do now? We can't stay any longer in this camp. We are only twenty helpless Jewish girls and sooner or later they will kill us. Suddenly it dawned on me. Quickly I woke up all twenty girls. We dressed quietly, packed our blankets and what little we had, and rushed out of the barrack to where the six hundred women were sleeping. We sneaked in among them and pretended to sleep.

Before the sun came out, we heard a whistle blow, and in no time the six hundred women, plus the twenty of us, marched in fives out of Zwodau. We kept our heads down, for fear someone would recognize us. But the transport had their own guards, so—surrounded by unfamiliar old guards with guns—we marched out into the cold morning of 20 April 1945.

The death march had begun. The first few days the twenty of us stayed together; we marched automatically during the day and slept at night in a barn or an open field. Once a day, the transport would stop in some village where the people would prepare a large kettle of soup and sometimes potatoes to feed us. We grabbed all we could, for we had been starved in Zwodau. The bowl of soup once a day was enough to satisfy our stomachs, but not so for all the six hundred other women.

A large group of these had come from Hungary. Only a few months before, from their warm beds, comfortable homes, and plenty of food, they had been sent directly to the concentration camps. Now they were herded like cattle on this march. With no food, no clothes suitable for the harsh climate, it was too sudden a change for them, and many died each day. During the night, a lorry would pick up the ones who couldn't walk anymore; and when we heard the gunfire, we knew they didn't have to suffer anymore.

We were now in the Sudetenland, the part of Czecho-slovakia occupied by the Germans since 1939. Every now and then we looked at the people in the villages and couldn't understand why they weren't helping us, why they weren't asking any questions. They saw our "zebra uniforms," they saw our "gamel" faces, they saw that we could hardly walk, yet they did nothing. One day we found ourselves in the center of a village.

Spontaneously, all of us began to run in all directions. The guards were dumbfounded. They couldn't do anything, for we were right in the midst of a civilian population. We ran like animals. We rushed into the stores, clutched food, anything we could lay our hands on, anything we could carry. Pola ran into a butcher store and we followed. We were still conscious of being together. She pulled a large chunk of bacon off the shelf, hid it under her blanket, and joined us. Finally the population of the village, frightened, shocked, pushed us back into the rows of the SS guards. They didn't want any part of this circus. From day to day, we became more and more like animals.

After this experience, the guards didn't stop in villages anymore. We didn't get a thing to eat. The women began to look for grass. We became wild with hunger. One day in the fields we found a hole in which potatoes and other vegetables had been stored for the winter. Like a flock of vultures, we tried to snatch at least one potato. Not one of us was strong enough to fight the Hungarians, who were really wild by now. Gienia, however, was lucky enough to seize a beet. Each of us took a bite. The beet, a red beet, tasted delicious. It was sour and juicy; it was fermented, for it had been frozen. After we ate the beet, all five of us felt sick and couldn't control the oncoming diarrhea.

The routine was to go over to the side of the road, and under the SS men's guns, squat to find relief. All through the day and night, the SS men had a good show. After the feast of raw potatoes and beets, on top of the bacon and some raw meat that the girls had stolen the day before, we were all sick. Diarrhea was the worst disease in camps always, but now it was a catastrophe. Gienia was becoming weaker every minute, and by the end of the day she couldn't walk anymore. Besides, there was no desire left in her to survive. Half-dead by now, she herself climbed onto the lorry. Anna saw her there, and quickly the two of us ran to the lorry and pulled her off before the guards could notice.

Gienia was tall and thin, but now she looked like a ghost. In her face, two holes appeared where eyes had been before. Her body was nothing but bones. She wouldn't walk anymore, she couldn't. We tied one blanket around her, put it under our arms, and pulled her along. It was a struggle, a tremendous struggle, for our strength had failed us, too. But we knew we had to save her.

That night we slept under the open skies. Before we closed our eyes, snow began to fall. It was a beautiful sight, the only clean thing we had seen for ages. We reached out for the snow and licked it. It felt good on our dry tongues. We were tired, yet couldn't go to sleep for fear we would never wake up again. We took turns waking up the ones who fell asleep. Mania, Pola, and Anna were lying next to me, or actually their shadows were, for there was nothing left of them. They looked like gamels—the last stage of a person in a concentration camp. Bones for the body, holes for the eyes, and inside, hardly anything left.

We could have escaped that night, perhaps, for there weren't too many guards left. Even they had left us. They couldn't take the cold and hunger either. But we knew there was no place to go. A few girls who had escaped a few days before had soon rejoined us; no one would keep them. There was no way to hide. Our destiny was foretold.

I prayed. I made up so many prayers these days. At first, I

used to pray for my mother and father and my little brother, Mojshele. Then, when he was taken into the gas chambers, I had to change my prayer. I prayed for his soul. When Mother was taken into the gas chambers of Auschwitz, I prayed for her soul. And I always prayed for her to watch over us, as I knew that in some way she would always watch over us.

I prayed for Father, but then hunger came and I prayed for food and for health for the four of us and the ones around us. But soon, my prayer included only the four of us. I prayed and prayed hard that the four of us would survive this war, that we would live to see the world, the free world. At length it seemed that God must have heard my prayer.

In the middle of the night, I saw a man appear in the woods that surrounded the field where we slept. I moved slowly towards him. I was afraid, but I wished to talk to him. He greeted me first. "The war is over, the Germans lost the war," he asserted in a firm voice.

I strained to hear as I drew closer. "What do you mean, the war is over?"

"Believe me, it won't be long." He rolled on the ground next to me, so no one would see him, and the music of his words flowed from his lips:" The Russians are coming from the east and the Americans from the west. The Germans are finished, there is nothing left. Any day now there will be a showdown and the end will be here, too, even here in these woods," he continued rejoicing. "Hitler committed suicide with his lover, Eva Braun," he continued as he drew in his breath quickly. "The Germans don't have a leader, they don't have men, they have nothing."

"But they still have us," I sullenly responded. "What an easy target."

"True, the guards have their orders and they will stick to them till the end. They don't even know what is going on. But listen, soon you will be in Czechoslovakia. It seems to me they are just leading you here and there; they can't do anything anymore. But the Czechs are different. They will keep you; they will save you or even take you from the guards if they have to." His eyes gleamed in the dark as he went on talking, and I listened. A shrill frost-wind reminded me of our grim circumstances. Suddenly fantasy and reality mingled in his words of freedom.

"Look," he insisted, "if you want to, you can come with me and I will find a place where I can hide you until the war ends." With this, he made a signal for departure.

I was reluctant to tell him about my sisters and Gienia and all the others whom I couldn't leave right now, not now when the end was so near.

It was almost dawn when he directed my gaze to the mountains directly ahead of us. They were on the Sudeten-Czech border where the Germans were still holding on in their last defense. I studied his wizened face as the words came once more: "It won't be long, believe me. Collect all the strength and willpower you have because you will soon be free." With these words he left, before the guards could see him.

My eyes followed him until he disappeared among the razor-sharp black shadows of the trees which lay across the phosphorescent greens of the morning snow. His body literally vanished into the woods. Was I dreaming? Was I losing my mind? Did it really happen, or was I imagining things? Was he real, or was he the Prophet Elijah, whom we had always waited for to appear on Passover night. When Father filled the cup of wine for the Prophet and opened the door, I could see him coming, I could feel his presence in the room. There was peace in our family, there was hope.

Now, shivering as I returned to the others in a world dominated by the cold glow of the late April sun, I asked myself: Could it be that the Prophet had shown himself to me on this forlorn April night? It could be Passover now; it used to be right about my birthday, I remembered. Was this Elijah who appeared to me and brought peace and hope?

I remembered my youth, my home, my family and friends, from long ago, and I tried to recapture the feeling—the feeling that I would last forever.

39 The morning sun shown for the last time on several bodies of those who had expired during the night. They were carefully put on the lorry, and under guard, we went into the woods where we covered their bodies with what little we could find that wasn't too frozen to lift. The lorry was thus emptied for the next shipment.

All through the awful task, I kept thinking about my prophet. In the meantime, we hugged our tatter-clad bodies, convulsing with hunger pains, to keep warm. We soon formed the familiar row of five with my sisters and Gienia, who was a little refreshed by the snow. Her body was dehydrated, and after she had licked a lot of snow, she had revived somewhat and could walk on her own.

I told them what I had seen the night before, and I reassured them that the war was coming to an end soon. Our eyes shone as we marched that day. We looked at each other and burst out laughing. What a sight: the bony cheeks where eyes rested, the flat chests, and the skeleton-like bodies. What a sight to laugh at, but we were still young and youth is a continual intoxication.

We glanced at our torn zebra uniforms, dirty and worn out by now. We hadn't had a change of clothes for six months. For six months we had worn this one and only dress, day and night. We didn't have any underwear. We were quite a sight. We had something to laugh about.

Then we remembered another time. Another age that we had lived in, when we had had clothes and food and families, when we frolicked and were happy. Was it possible there was a time when we were able to race through the woods and come into a warm, clean home? Dante once said, "There is no greater pain, than in misery, to remember happy times." I didn't think he really knew what misery was.

We could almost feel the warmth. We could almost taste the food. The desire to feel it all, to experience the sensation of living, to see our dear ones again was so strong that it helped us to be insusceptible to all the brutality and the forces around us.

It was on the following night, 1 May 1945, that we put our heads down to sleep for the last time under the guard of the German SS.

We were in a large barn far up in the mountains. It seemed like the end of the world. Nothing in sight but fields and woods. In the morning, when the sun's rays came slanting through the dustholes of the barn, there appeared hundreds of helpless shadows lying on the wide-planked floor.

I couldn't get up. I imagined very sick people must have felt like this, when in their minds, they felt like getting up, lifting their heads, their numb arms and useless legs, but they couldn't. Their bodies wouldn't move. They were paralyzed. This was exactly how I felt on that morning in May. I couldn't even sit up. I couldn't raise my head. My eyes wandered about looking for my sisters. I didn't want them to see me in this condition. It had to pass quickly. It had to.

Then I saw Anna sitting up; I saw Mania, too. But Pola? Pola, I thought I heard her crying. Yes, Pola was crying.

"I can't, I can't, I can't get up anymore. I just want to die," she whimpered weakly. Anna looked at me with her large brown eyes and suddenly started to cry. She realized something was wrong with me. She began plaintively, "What are we going to do? Oh, no, not you, Ruth, Ruth!"

"Listen, you go ahead. Pola and I will stay here. The war will be over soon anyhow," I said quietly with effort.

"We aren't going either. We shall all stay with you," Mania and Anna declared. And Gienia, poor Gienia, echoed them too.

"You saved my life, remember? I don't care what happens to me. I shall stay with you," she cried.

A woman next to me whose name I shall always remember, a Mrs. Tyras, handed me a few kernels of wheat. "Here, here, take this." She had found it somewhere in the barn.

I hadn't had any food in my mouth except snow for several days, and my tongue was dry. The kernels of wheat looked like manna from heaven. I took one, two, three in my mouth. I kept the wheat on my tongue awhile, I held it in my mouth, I ate the kernels. She then gave me a handful. I exerted myself, reached toward Pola and handed her a few kernels too. She ate it vigorously. I now found I could move slowly. I raised my head unsteadily. Pola gazed dully around the barn; she couldn't raise herself up at all but pointed to Mania. She said in a hushed tone, "Here, look, there is a hole under this barn. We can all hide in it. The war will be over soon."

I listened in disbelief as the soft words came from Pola's parched throat. My dear, precious Pola, my bitter Pola had no bitterness anymore. She had said the war would be over soon? Did she really feel it, or did she mean the war would be over for her? I could dimly see that she looked as if at any moment she might draw her last breath and would be gone forever. No more grief and misery for her. And I myself felt the same way. I felt life withering in my gaunt body.

As I turned my head, I saw the hole in the ground. Before most of the women got up, we started climbing under the barn. The hole was small, but our skeleton bodies could just fit through.

We fumbled to climb in. First Anna, then we pushed Pola in; she still couldn't walk. Then Mania and Gienia, and finally, Mrs. Tyras helped me make my way in. Her friendly hands covered the hole with what little hay she could find and she wished us luck. She was going to continue the journey until the end of the war came. She wasn't going to endanger her life now at the end. It was a known procedure that after each night the Germans counted and recounted—the dead and the living. If someone was missing, they searched and searched until they could satisfy their brutish desire to kill.

We had no choice. We couldn't continue to walk and couldn't face going to the lorry. We had one chance for survival and that was to hide; if we were lucky, the Germans wouldn't find us. We could then escape to Czechoslovakia, according to my prophet, and from there to freedom.

We lay on our stomachs. We heard moving bodies above us. After a long while, all was quiet. Then suddenly, we heard the loud noises of the SS men searching, stepping everywhere, looking. The hay in front of our hole was moved by a gun.

We all stopped breathing. If he removed one more bit of hay, he would see the hole and start searching closer. We all died in that short moment. Then he moved; he walked away. We all took a deep breath, lying very still without uttering a word to each other.

In addition to our terror at being discovered, one after

another of us began to have diarrhea. There was no room to move. The smell was suffocating. We touched each other every now and then to make sure we were all alive.

Finally, unable to breathe anymore, we decided we could only survive if we left our hiding place. It was almost dark when we cautiously emerged, more like violet shades than human beings, from the hole. The barn was quiet. We found some hay and wiped our bodies and our soiled dresses. Although hardly anything could be seen, we decided to creep through a back way for fear the owners of the barn would turn us in.

Forcing a board aside in the back part of the barn, we escaped through the opening. We were in a field. The gentle haze of the evening dusk revealed tender blades of new grass coming through the ground. The five of us were all standing. We studied each other closely and scarcely believed it possible; only yesterday morning Pola and I had found it impossible to get up and now, now we were ready to run for freedom. We felt an immediate sensation of space, an impulse to experience the physical joy of life, a longing to be spontaneous once more. The thought of freedom, like a flood-tide, surged through us and stimulated our strained, mute bodies.

Just over the brow of a hill, bells were ringing. A church must have been in the distance. We moved hurriedly toward it with an unexpected vitality. Perhaps the worshippers in it would give us a hearty welcome and help us. Those who believe surely must be kindly; they won't let us die, not now when the war was almost over. Besides, we knew that Czechoslovakia was nearby; and the church might very well be in Czechoslovakia for all we knew.

We ran.

Suddenly we saw a light, a farm. We had to stop, we had to wash ourselves because the diarrhea was killing us and we needed water to drink. Or perhaps we could even get some food.

We made our way to the farmhouse. A woman came out. We asked for water and she showed us the pipe outside. We asked if we could have some food and she said she had some soup left over from dinner. She looked at us, didn't say a word, but didn't let us into the house either.

We were frightened, too, frightened that she might send a

message to our transport. They must have passed by her farm also. We drank all the water we could, washed our buttocks that were terribly sore by now, swallowed the small portion of soup we received and, without a word, hastened away.

We continued to race. By now it was night. We didn't know where we were. We followed the moon. Once over a hill, we noticed lights. It looked like a village. We walked towards it hoping to get there before everyone had gone to sleep. The tiny village looked like a bird's nest. We decided to rest there. We knocked on a door.

A short, heavy woman opened the door for us. "I don't have any bread, but I will be happy to boil some potatoes for you," she said. As she busied herself, she explained: "My husband and my son were killed in the war. I am all alone with my daughter. She is away working." We were glad there were no men around.

We sat silently around her kitchen table. We were in a home. The warmth penetrated our cold bodies. We didn't say a word as she placed the pot of potatoes on the stove. She fed more wood into the stove. We waited in silence. We stared at the pot and our tongues were moving, our stomachs were rumbling. When the potatoes were ready, she poured them piping hot and steaming into a bowl and began to peel them. But before she could get very far, we started grabbing and eating them.

"A boiled potato, I shall never eat a boiled potato," the words rang in my ears. We had our fill of boiled potatoes and then we were each given a glass of milk. The woman stared in amazement, and without a word, let us eat and drink like animals. Food, we were able to eat food. We were in a home, a warm, friendly home. She let us sleep in the kitchen. We slept that night.

The next day, much to our distress, we all developed diarrhea worse than before. The food plainly didn't agree with us. We weren't used to food anymore. Her toilet was an outhouse. We dashed to it, one after another, covering any evidences of the diarrhea along the pathway with grass so the woman wouldn't see it. If she suspected we might have typhus, she would drive us away. We couldn't afford to leave her warm home. Besides, we learned from her that the Germans were still fighting in the woods. Furthermore, she thought that the

Americans were some sort of giants, and the war would certainly end any day now. She had even heard that Czechoslovakia was free already.

Because we didn't wish to be seen in our zebra uniforms any longer, we begged our generous benefactor for a couple of sheets and a few old blankets. We promised to pay for them when the Americans came. We assured her we had uncles in America and they would gladly reimburse her amply for them.

Mania started cutting and each of us, needle in hand, started sewing: blouses from the sheets, skirts from the blankets. We didn't need much material since we were all so skinny. It was not long before we paraded in our beautiful outfits (perhaps the most beautiful outfit I shall ever possess).

On the third day of our stay, there was an unexpected visit from the village elder. The authorities had learned that she had some young women, and we were to go to work or leave the area.

We listened to this in terror. We couldn't risk going through registration and out to work again. We knew how thorough the Germans were. We had to run again. In detail, we explained we were only Polish girls, not Jewish, and that we had been working in Germany. This district was on our way home.

Our understanding hostess packed a bag of boiled potatoes for us, and in the evening we left. As quickly as we could, we safely made our way through the very same woods where the Americans were fighting the Germans. All through the forest there were mines and other traps. That night, we slept under the clear skies of May. In the morning, rested and no longer hungry but still having diarrhea, we continued to walk cautiously through the forest. The sky was clear and the sun was high as we reached the small village in Czechoslovakia on 7 May 1945. A group of women were gathered in a courtyard. We heard them shout:

"The Americans are coming! The Americans are coming!"

Epilogue

Shortly after liberation I started working for the United Nations Relief and Rehabilitation Administration in Tirschenreuth, Germany. On 1 December 1945 I went on a field trip to Schwandorf, where I met a number of young doctors who had survived the war. One of them was Henry Rubinstein, who applied for a job in the Displaced Persons' Hospital in Tirschenreuth. I found an apartment for him, and within a few days he moved to our town.

Dr. Rubinstein kept asking about his mother and it soon became apparent that he was the son of Mrs. B. in this story. We were married 19 March 1946; we still are.